SEAL OF THE SUPREME COURT OF THE UNITED STATES

For ██████████ with
appreciation and
good wishes —

Sandra O'Connor

With appreciation to ██████████
for your friendship and many Kindness to us,

██████████

██████

BY SANDRA DAY O'CONNOR

Lazy B

The Majesty of the Law

Out of Order

Chico

Finding Susie

OUT *of* ORDER

OUT
of
ORDER

—— // ——

*Stories from the History of
the Supreme Court*

SANDRA DAY
O'CONNOR

RANDOM HOUSE / NEW YORK

Published in the United States by Random House,
an imprint of The Random House Publishing Group,
a division of Random House, Inc., New York.

RANDOM HOUSE and colophon are registered trademarks
of Random House, Inc.

Grateful acknowledgment is made to Hal Leonard Corporation
for permission to reprint an excerpt from "Ac-cent-tchu-ate the Positive"
from the motion picture *Here Come the Waves,* lyric by Johnny Mercer and
music by Harold Arlen, copyright © 1944 (renewed) Harwin Music Co.
All rights reserved. Reprinted by permission of
Hal Leonard Corporation.

LIBRARY OF CONGRESS CATALOGING-IN-PUBLICATION DATA

O'Connor, Sandra Day.
Out of order: stories from the history of the Supreme Court /
Sandra Day O'Connor.
p. cm.
Includes bibliographical references and index.
ISBN 978–0-8129–9392–9
eISBN 978–0-8129–9393–6
1. United States. Supreme Court—History.   2. United States.
Supreme Court—Anecdotes.   3. Courts of last resort—United States—
History.   4. Courts of last resort—United States—Anecdotes.   I. Title.
KF8742.O276 2013 347.73'2609—dc23 2012025708

Printed in the United States of America on acid-free paper

www.atrandom.com

6897

Book design by Susan Turner

This book is dedicated to my law clerks, who helped me learn, research, and appreciate the Court's history, and to Craig Joyce, who encouraged me to write this book, *Out of Order.*

It is written after my retirement as a Supreme Court Justice and with the benefit of twenty-five years of service on the Court. I began my service there with admiration for the Court but trepidation about my role as a Justice. I look back on it with continued admiration for the Court and for my colleagues there. The Court is as much needed today as it was when it began. Long may it survive!

CONTENTS

INTRODUCTION

O N SEPTEMBER 25, 1981, MY FIRST DAY AS A UNITED STATES Supreme Court Justice, I walked up the steps to the Supreme Court for only the second time. Decades before, I had visited the Court with my husband, John, as a simple tourist while John was attending army training in neighboring Virginia. It was a Saturday and the Court was closed. I snapped a picture of John as he stood on the marble steps. I remember thinking that that was the closest I would ever get to the Supreme Court. I could not have fathomed that, years later, I would walk down those marble steps as a member of the Supreme Court and serve for nearly twenty-five years.

The Supreme Court Building is an awe-inspiring sight. Many a visitor each year is stopped in his or her tracks by the grandeur and solemnity of the white marble staircase and the soaring inscription on the Court's façade, EQUAL JUSTICE UNDER LAW. An inspiring and profound image of permanence and continuity, the Court stands as a symbol of our commitment as a society to the rule of law. It stands for our Founding Fathers' uniquely American vision of an independent judiciary, in which judges and the

Chief Justice Warren Burger escorts Justice Sandra Day O'Connor down the front steps of the Supreme Court on the day of her investiture.

Court would stand alone, independent and not beholden to the will of political majorities in their interpretation of the laws and the Constitution.

Most people would say that the reasons for having the legislative and executive branches of government are obvious. After all, we need legislators to make the laws, and an executive to enforce them. The Framers of the Constitution created a powerful national government to reflect and implement popular will. With the revolution against monarchical rule fresh in mind, the Framers saw legislatures of elected representatives answerable to the people as "the heart and soul of any system of truly 'republican' government."[1] And while memories of King George III's tyrannical reign fostered distrust of executive power, the Framers also recognized the need for a vigorous presidency rooted in the will of the people. Under the Articles of Confederation, a weak national government had struggled to provide for the country's needs and speak for the people with a single voice.

But why did the Framers envision for the new government a judicial branch whose members, unlike those of the legislative and executive branches, would be unelected? And why was a *federal* judiciary necessary, given the extensive system of state courts in existence at the time of the Founding? Today, state courts can still decide nearly any issue of law and they still handle the bulk of the nation's cases.

The Framers wished to create an independent federal judiciary because they knew that the new national political branches could not be left unchecked. Our congressmen and President serve as elected representatives. In that role, they are supposed to speak for and answer to the people. For that reason, the Framers did not rely on the political branches to protect minority groups with less popular, more marginal interests. And so they assigned federal courts primary responsibility in guarding against the overreaching and excesses of the political branches, recognizing the benefits of a judiciary that functions as an "outsider" to the system of majority will.

The majestic building on One First Street in our nation's capital stands as a monument to our Founding Fathers' vision. Erected across the street from the Capitol, and across town from the White House, the building stands as a physical testament to the Court's status as an independent, coequal branch of government. The Supreme Court today regularly reviews the legality of laws passed by Congress and enforced by the executive branch. And from time to time, the Justices find themselves compelled by the law to strike down invalid government action by the political branches. The Court's decisions today, though often the subject of public criticism, are followed and adhered to even by those who disagree. Indeed, the Court has withstood tests of its authority on matters as controversial as school desegregation in the 1950s and the conduct of the War on Terror in the first decade of this century.

I had the privilege of serving on the Supreme Court from 1981 until 2006, as it confronted issues running the gamut from states' rights and race-based affirmative action to a defendant's right to effective assistance of counsel. My colleagues and I always strove to reach the right answers, and I hope that we did. We were able to resolve tough questions in an atmosphere insulated as far as possible from political pressures.

In those years, I also grew accustomed to many things that facilitate the important role that the Supreme Court plays in our system of government. For instance, it went without saying that, at any given time, I had eight colleagues who were well trained in the law, committed to their jobs, and willing to spend years, even decades, as officers of the Court. It also went without saying that the Term followed a regular schedule, that we had personal chambers in which we could work, and that we had available clerk's and reporter's offices that ran like well-oiled machines. The staff at the Court are first-rate professionals, and I had my pick of wonderful, talented law clerks to assist in my chambers each year.

This was not always the case. Far from it. So many aspects of the Court were shaped and developed little by little, year by year, person by person. The Court was a daring, bold, but risky political experiment, and its beginnings were modest and uncertain.

In reflecting on the Court's humble early days, it is striking to note how dramatically the Court and its practices have evolved and how so much of that evolution was born of struggle and serendipity. I find it remarkable to reflect on how, for many decades of the Court's early existence, so much of what we take for granted was steeped in uncertainty. The many Justices who have come and gone have made contributions—dramatic and subtle, renowned and lesser known—to not only the law, but the institution and its internal operations.

In this book, I hope to shed light on some of those transformations. This book offers snapshots of the people and events that reflect the Court's evolution and journey.

From the array of characters who have served as Justices, to the law clerks who have aided them, the advocates who have argued before them, and the staff who have worked behind the scenes, the makeup of the community of the Court has changed dramatically. Just consider the criteria that Presidents have laid out for Supreme Court nominees. President George Washington was looking for men who were strong supporters of the Federalist cause and the Constitution, who had served in the Revolution, who were active in the political life of their states, and who had the blessing of well-known Federalists—the party that favored a strong national government. President Obama has stated that he looks for men and women with "a sharp and independent mind," who understand "that justice isn't about some abstract legal theory," and who "identif[y] with people's hopes and struggles as an essential ingredient for arriving at just decisions and outcomes."[2]

The life of a Justice is very different, too. In 1791, Justice John Rutledge left the job less than two years into it because, frustrated by the Court's lack of activity, he preferred to serve on a lower court, the South Carolina Court of Common Pleas. In the early days, it was also not unusual for Justices to leave the Court to assume or run for political office. Justice David Davis resigned in 1877 to take a seat in the Senate and Justice Charles Evan Hughes resigned in 1916 to run for President. (He returned to the Court in 1930.) Today, however, we are accustomed to having Justices serve out a full life tenure. And whereas the thought of seeing a woman Justice was hard to fathom until 1981, today we have three women sitting on the Supreme Court bench, left, right, and center.

In the early days, convincing good candidates that the job of a Justice was worthwhile was difficult. In the era of "circuit-riding," Justices crisscrossed the country to preside over lower-court trials and appeals. Many Justices traveled up to ten thousand miles per year by horseback, stagecoach, and riverboat, enduring often hazardous conditions on the road.[3] The Court did not even have a permanent home until 1935. In its early days, the Court moved from the Exchange Building in New York to the State House in Philadelphia to various short-term homes around Washington, D.C. Today, with no obligation to ride circuit, the Justices enjoy their impressive and comfortable quarters at One First Street.

The everyday operations and customs of the Court have evolved as well. The early Court had few cases on its docket. In the days of Chief Justice John Marshall, the Court often sat for cases for only six weeks.[4] Today, the Supreme Court Term runs for nine months, from October each year through the following June. The Court's role in picking the cases it hears has also changed dramatically. In the late nineteenth century, the Court's docket was inundated with mandatory appeals—cases that the Justices were at least technically obliged to decide on the merits, regardless of their importance or the urgency for review. Today, the Court uses its discretion to select a small subset of cases from approximately eight thousand appeals, known as "petitions for certiorari," filed each year.

Those who practice before the Supreme Court also face a very different scene. Early oral advocates were unconstrained by any time limitations, or indeed, any real rules of practice. When they presented their arguments, they were "heard in silence for hours, without being stopped or interrupted" by the Justices.[5] High-style oratory inspired by Demosthenes and Cicero was in fashion and oral arguments could last for ten days.[6] Today, oral advocates are strictly limited to thirty minutes of argument time per side. Classical oral exposition is discouraged, and advocates are lucky if they get more than two unbroken sentences out of their mouths before the Justices interject with difficult questions.

The Court's dramatic evolution over time is humbling to review. In my nearly twenty-five years on the Supreme Court, I was always cognizant of how my tenure, lengthy as it was, was but one small part of a rich and unfolding tapestry. Each Justice plays merely a supporting role in the Court's ongoing narrative, and each Justice's experience is but a snapshot in time. I am reminded of this each time I walk through the Court and admire the succession of portraits—some famous, some less known—gracing its hallways. The Court as it exists today reflects the contributions of those who devoted their lives to it.

When I retired from the Court, I found myself increasingly being asked by people across the country and across the world for my "insider" perspective on the Court and its goings-on. Very often, the inquirer would have recently seen a newspaper editorial about a controversial case or read some supposed "tell-all" book on the Court. I would always answer that my years of service were a privilege, that I had great affection for my colleagues, and that the Justices strive to reach the right result in each case. I came to realize that what I wished to convey above all was my understanding of how the Court evolved, and how it represents so much more than what the day's headlines can capture. It embodies the bold vision of the Framers of our Constitution, a triumph of the rule of law, and the culmination of the hard work, risks, and sacrifices of many people.

I wanted to write about aspects of the Court's rich heritage that interested and inspired me. Hence this book. Only when we reflect on the Court's journey as a whole can we truly appreciate the remarkable feat of our Founding Fathers and the remarkable accomplishments of our thriving federal judiciary.

OUT *of* ORDER

LOOMING LARGE

*Historic Intersections of the President
and the Supreme Court*

———//———

THE ROLE OF THE JUDICIAL BRANCH IN OUR SYSTEM OF GOV-
ernment differs markedly from that of the executive
branch. Each shoulders substantial powers and obligations under the Constitution. Whereas the Executive enforces
the law, however, the Supreme Court interprets the law and has
no power to command obedience or appropriate funds to enforce its orders. Whereas the President is elected by the people
and serves for limited terms, federal judges are appointed by the
President with the advice and consent of the Senate and serve for
life. Whereas the Executive reflects the political will of the majority, the judiciary is designed to check assertions of power by the
political branches. It thus comes as little surprise that throughout
history, the Executive and the Supreme Court have intersected,
overlapped, and even clashed.

A story is told that William Howard Taft once found himself
stranded at a small country railroad station. Informed that the
express train would stop only for a large group of passengers,
Taft wired the conductor: "Stop at Hicksville. Large party waiting to catch train." When the train stopped, Taft boarded, alone.

He then turned to the confused conductor. "You can go on ahead," he declared. "*I* am the large party."

We laugh at that story because we remember that Mr. Taft, at his heaviest, tipped the scales at over three hundred pounds. But as the twenty-seventh President of the United States and the tenth Chief Justice of the United States, he also was the only person ever to have tipped the scales by holding both of those incredibly "large" offices—experiencing firsthand the responsibility of heading two of the most significant institutions in the free world. His time in these two roles put him on two different sides of the same constitutional coin.

Indeed, our remarkable Constitution recognizes the individual "largeness" of these governmental bodies while acknowledging that their relative strengths will at times coexist, at times collide, and nearly always manage to carry out the will of the majority while safeguarding the rights of the minority. A look at the dynamic between these two institutions speaks volumes about the genius of our Constitution.

To FIND AN EXAMPLE of the judiciary and the presidency surviving the collision of two larger-than-life personalities, we need not travel very far into the early days of our republic. Second cousins John Marshall and Thomas Jefferson were anything but the kissing kind. Indeed, their relationship was privately nasty and publicly only slightly better. Their exchanges—well documented, but not well-mannered—planted the seeds for an all-out war over the proper role of the judiciary vis-à-vis the other branches of government, and set the trajectory of constitutional law as we know it today.

Jefferson almost was not our third president, coming to the post only after the House of Representatives broke an electoral tie vote in his race with Aaron Burr. Marshall almost was not our fourth Chief Justice, receiving the nomination from John Adams only after first choice John Jay declined reappointment. But once fate brought them to their respective positions of authority in 1801, Jefferson and Marshall came to blows in ways that put even today's climate of political acrimony to shame.

Early in his administration, Jefferson attempted to have Marshall impeached. He accused him of "irregular and censurable" behavior.[1] In Marshall's hands, Jefferson lamented, "the law is nothing more than an ambiguous text, to be explained by his sophistry into any meaning which may subserve his personal malice."[2] He spoke vehemently of his bitter disappointment in his own appointees to the Supreme Court, calling them "lazy" and weak for not standing up to the "crafty chief judge."[3]

Marshall, in turn, labeled Jefferson "totally unfit" for the presidency.[4]

Jefferson called the Chief Justice a man "of lax lounging manners . . . and a profound hypocrisy."[5] Over time, these two actors played out a rather hateful drama, rooted in personal animus and fundamental disagreement as to the proper role of government and the appropriate balance between the judicial and executive branches.

History teaches us that it was Marshall's decision in *Marbury v. Madison* that permanently legitimated and strengthened the Supreme Court and that gave the Chief Justice his least obvious but perhaps greatest victory over the President. Many say that that case, which came to stand for the authority of the Court to review the acts of the political branches, might as well have been captioned *Marshall v. Jefferson*.

Here is what happened. In the watershed 1800 election, Marshall's Federalist Party lost control of the executive and the legislative branches to Jefferson's Republicans, and in an effort to retain some presence in government, the Federalists decided to pack the Court before they left office. President Adams appointed Marshall, then the secretary of state, as Chief Justice, and Congress passed a number of pieces of legislation to restructure the

Portrait of Chief Justice John Marshall.   *Portrait of William Marbury.*

court system and provide the lame-duck Senate and outgoing President Adams with many new positions to fill. Adams filled them—or thought he did—through a series of midnight appointments.

But Jefferson fought back. When he took office as President, he refused to deliver the commissions of some of the Adams appointees. When William Marbury, an appointed judge who didn't get his commission, sought a court order compelling the administration to deliver his commission, the case made its way to the Supreme Court.

Chief Justice Marshall, to the surprise of many, denied the order that would have forced his nemesis Jefferson to issue the judicial commissions. That might have seemed like a victory for the new President.

But the "victory" that Marshall handed to Jefferson came with a silver lining for the Court and for himself. Marshall and the Court denied the order to grant Marbury's commission on the grounds that the part of the Judiciary Act of 1789 that had given the Supreme Court the power to issue such orders was contrary to the Constitution.

Writing for a unanimous Court in 1803, Marshall declared "that courts, as well as other departments, are bound by [the Constitution]" and, more important, that it is "emphatically the province and duty of the judicial department" to say what the Constitution means.[6]

In one fell swoop, Marshall gave up a small power that Congress had conferred upon the Court and took in exchange an even larger, overarching power—to examine and decide the ultimate constitutionality of all acts of Congress that one challenged in Court. Despite the vehement disagreement of his cousin Thomas Jefferson, this bold assertion by John Marshall about the power of the Court has survived as the final and official answer to this day. Today, portraits of Marbury and Madison hang in the Justices' private dining room in the Supreme Court—an ongoing reminder of how the Court established its role as a coequal branch.

The lessons to be learned from the story of Jefferson and Marshall are many. It is the story of a government that develops and evolves, that grows and changes, over time. It is the story of large institutions competing and accommodating and evolving in ways that may both amaze and alarm us. Perhaps even more significant, it is a story that begins a distinctively human thread that is woven throughout all of the Court's history: The judiciary and the presidency are inhabited by real people, with real emotions, real foibles, and a very real—if sometimes conflicting—commitment to doing what is right.

A SECOND HISTORIC MOMENT of interaction between the presidency and the judiciary stars President Abraham Lincoln and Chief Justice Roger Brooke Taney. It represents one of the only times a sitting president has deliberately defied a direct court order.

In the early days of the Civil War, the fragile American nation faced serious threats from within. The Southern states had broken away, and European powers were poised to intervene, to divide the young nation permanently into Union and Confederacy. The war posed another sort of danger—a danger less obvious, perhaps, than columns of soldiers marching through the countryside but far more insidious to a nation "conceived in Liberty." It was the danger that a government at war might use its extraordinary powers to stamp out political opposition. In April 1861, a trainload of Union soldiers passed through Baltimore en route to Washington, summoned to man the defensive fortifications around the capital. They were greeted by an angry mob of Southern sympathizers and had to fight their way across Baltimore to reach the station where their train to Washington was waiting. Later that night, local authorities who favored the South sabotaged the bridges and telegraph lines connecting Baltimore and Washington. Their story was that they feared the soldiers might return and seek revenge for the riot, but their actions endangered the Union by cutting off the two critical cities.

With Congress out of session, President Lincoln found himself alone in the capital with the rebel army closing in from the south and an apparent insurrection brewing to the north. Taking action as commander in chief, he directed local military leaders to secure the railroad line from Washington to Philadelphia, and allowed them to suspend "habeas corpus" in that pursuit. Sometimes called the "Great Writ," habeas corpus is the relief that a prisoner requests from a court when they are seeking release from unlawful detention. Thus, by suspending the writ, Lincoln was effectively permitting the Union army to arrest civilians without a warrant, without probable cause, without a speedy jury trial—indeed, without any process at all. Mr. John Merryman, a member of the Maryland legislature who had been recruiting rebel soldiers, was arrested by a Union general under this scheme, and hauled off to Fort McHenry in Baltimore Harbor.

In those days, Justices of the Supreme Court were still "riding

circuit"—literally riding their horses in circles around the country to sit as federal judges on lower courts in addition to their
service on the Supreme Court. Accordingly, Merryman's plea for
relief from detention was directed at his local circuit judge, who
happened to be Chief Justice Taney. Taney was no friend of Lincoln's administration. Upon receiving Merryman's plea, he ordered Merryman's jailer at Fort McHenry to bring Merryman to
the court, a command that is the essence of habeas corpus relief.
(Habeas corpus literally translates as something like "present the
body.") The commander refused, sending Taney an aide instead
with the message that the President had authorized the colonel
to suspend the Great Writ.

Taney was livid. He wrote an incendiary decision, holding
that it was for Congress, and only Congress, to suspend the writ
of habeas corpus. The President's job was only to see that the
laws be "faithfully executed."[7] He could not change the nation's
laws to suit his interests, even in times of war.

Lincoln gave Taney no response until Congress reconvened a
month later, on July 4. At that point, he let loose his own barrage
of heated rhetoric, some of which still echoes to this day. Lincoln
noted that the Confederacy had renounced the Constitution
under which Taney had purported to invalidate the President's
actions and argued that, had he not acted when he did, Washington would have fallen into Southern hands and there would have
been no Congress to respond to the rebellion. He famously asked:
"Are all the laws, but one, to go unexecuted, and the government
itself go to pieces, lest that one be violated?"[8]

In any event, Congress retroactively approved Lincoln's decision to suspend the writ and Merryman was never released.
Scholars remain divided on the question whether Lincoln had the
power to act as he did under the Constitution's "Suspension
Clause," which says only that habeas corpus shall not be suspended "except when in cases of rebellion or invasion the public
safety may require it." Because it appears in the part of the Con-

stitution that deals with Congress's powers, some say suspension is for Congress alone. On the other hand, because it appears to permit suspension "in cases of rebellion" and it is the President who never takes a recess and must always safeguard the nation as commander in chief, others say that Lincoln did only what the Constitution permits. This is not the place for me to offer my own views in that debate. Suffice it to say that Lincoln won the debate in his own day, especially because Congress itself eventually sided with him in March 1863. And to his immense credit, Lincoln did *not* use this express authorization from Congress to trample on the civil liberties that the writ of habeas corpus was meant to protect.

Recent historical studies have made clear that Lincoln never tried to suppress political dissent, and always understood that a democracy grows stronger by allowing the people to voice their opposition to government, even in the midst of war. He appreciated that the strength of the Union lay not only in force of arms but in the liberties that were guaranteed by the open, and sometimes heated, exchange of ideas. And he no doubt would have been pleased to know that, soon after his assassination and the conclusion of the war, his predictions that habeas corpus would quickly be reinstated came to pass. In his words, "what constitutes the bulwark of our own liberty and independence" is "not our frowning battlements, our bristling sea coasts, the guns of our war steamers, or the strength of our gallant and disciplined army," but rather "the love of liberty" and "the preservation of the spirit which prizes liberty as the heritage of men, in all lands, everywhere."[9]

In this way, what might otherwise be remembered as a clash between these two "large" historic figures can be seen as a moment of large respect for the rule of law by both the President and the Chief Justice. The constitutional debate sparked by Lincoln and Taney rages on even now. But we would do well to look beyond the conflict and to appreciate the character of the men behind the story. Their sincere, even if conflicting, examples of dedication to principle—and to the people of a struggling nation—loom large to this day.

A THIRD, WELL-KNOWN account of the intersection between the large scopes of influence of the judiciary and the presidency is found in the story of President Franklin D. Roosevelt's Judiciary Reorganization Bill of 1937. Roosevelt's bill, more commonly known as the "court-packing plan," would have increased the number of Supreme Court Justices from nine to fifteen. Indeed, the current head count of nine is engraved neither in stone nor in the Constitution, and could very well have turned out differently had Roosevelt had his way.

President Roosevelt cited the heavy workload and advancing age of many of the Supreme Court's then-sitting Justices to justify his proposed increase in ranks. However, historians have long focused on what is widely believed to be the real reason for his plan: According to accepted wisdom, Roosevelt was more than a little annoyed at the current Justices. The Court had been giving a thumbs-down to so much of his "New Deal" legislation— various economic programs targeted at redressing the aftermath of the Great Depression.

To be fair, Roosevelt wasn't just imagining things. In the 140 years between 1790 and 1930, the Court had overruled only sixty acts of Congress. Yet during Roosevelt's first term alone, 1933– 37, the Court overruled twelve acts—and some of those were the President's favorites! Among other laws, the Court struck down legislation including the National Industrial Recovery Act, the Railroad Retirement Act, and the Agricultural Adjustment Act. In fact, on the aptly named "Black Monday," May 27, 1935, the Court struck down three pieces of legislation all at once. At that pace, President Roosevelt feared the Court would soon dismantle his New Deal reforms completely.

His clever proposal was to get Congress to pass a bill that

would let him appoint a new Justice every time a Justice turned seventy years old. Coincidentally (or not), six members of the Court were over seventy at the time. The plan, in other words, would have ensured the President various changes in the makeup of the Court.

In the end, President Roosevelt's court-packing plan failed to pass. The plan faced enormous public opposition because it was perceived as an effort to stack the Court with champions of his agenda and stifle its independence. A critical supporter of the legislation, moreover, Senate Majority Leader Joseph T. Robinson, unexpectedly died mere weeks into the Senate's floor debate of the bill. The Senate voted to send the bill back to the Senate Judiciary Committee, and the bill was soon scrubbed of the provisions providing for additional Justices.

And so the Court survived what many viewed as one of the greatest crises of its history. It emerged larger in influence, if not in numbers, and more keenly aware of its sometimes tenuous, but always interesting, relationship with the presidency.

PERHAPS THE MOST SIGNIFICANT story to be told on this subject—at least in terms of the legal precedent with which it provided us—took place in April 1952, during the Korean War. It featured President Harry S. Truman, a steelworkers' union, and Justice Robert Jackson. Justice Jackson had as a law clerk at the time a bright young lawyer by the name of William H. Rehnquist—the future Chief Justice.

At this critical time in the Korean War effort, the steel industry and the United Steelworkers Union had reached an impasse in their negotiations. A looming strike by more than six hundred thousand workers threatened to cripple the production of weapons and, in Truman's eyes, endanger American troops serving in Korea. Ever sympathetic to the steelworkers, President Truman had worked for months to prevent the strike, and he turned to his advisers for counsel. The recommendation? To seize the steel mills, forcing the companies and labor to return to the bargaining table and management to retract what Truman viewed as "outrageous" demands for regulatory approval of significant price-per-ton increases. The President took the advice. Just hours before the scheduled strike, in an impromptu press conference, he stared into the camera and announced on national television that he would order his secretary of commerce, Charles Sawyer, to take over the mills and keep them running.

The President's advisers, it turned out, had not counted on the courts entering the fray. Historical documents now tell us that they counseled him that the odds were low that the judiciary would involve itself in such a hot-button issue. They believed that the short-lived seizure would serve its designed purpose of nudging labor and management into more productive talks, and have no wider ramifications. What resulted was something much larger: an act that would forever impact the American presidency and a watershed Supreme Court decision defining the limits of presidential power.

It began with Judge David Pine of the U.S. District Court for the District of Columbia. Judge Pine, to the surprise of the administration—and even the steel companies' own lawyers—declared the seizure unconstitutional, saying there was "utter and complete lack of authoritative support" for a President's seizure of private businesses. The U.S. Court of Appeals for the D.C. Circuit then entered a stay.

Finally, the Supreme Court heard expedited arguments. The government emphasized that the President's seizure was on sound historical footing, noting wartime government seizures of private property from the Revolutionary War and War of 1812 through Lincoln's Emancipation Proclamation and World Wars I and II. The steel industry, on the other hand, argued that the President did not have any power to seize private property without express authorization from Congress.

A blindfolded Justice in his judicial robes labeled "Supreme Court" holds a scale with his left hand. On the left scale is a rolled document labeled "U.S. Constitution" balanced against President Truman sitting on the right side. The side with the Constitution is obviously heavier. This cartoon refers to the Steel Seizure Case in 1952.

In its decision in *Youngstown Sheet & Tube v. Sawyer*,[10] the Court echoed the district court's rebuke of President Truman: He had, indeed, exceeded his powers under the Constitution. Writing for the majority, Justice Hugo Black rejected the administration's argument that in a time of war, the President could exercise his emergency powers in so broad a fashion as to make them almost boundless.

The most enduring opinion in the case, however, was the concurrence penned by Justice Jackson—an insightful exegesis of the issue of presidential powers. Justice Jackson endeavored to avoid drawing any rigid lines between Congress's power and the President's power. Instead, he provided a three-part framework for considering the relationship between presidential powers, congressional powers, and the Court's level of deference. First, when the President acts with Congress's approval, the President's power is at its zenith; in such cases, the judiciary will rarely push back on the President's exercise of power. Second, when the President acts without congressional approval or disapproval, this represents a "twilight" area where the rigor of judicial review is heightened. Third, when the President acts amid congressional disapproval, his power is at its "lowest ebb," and the Court will usually invalidate the action. In Justice Jackson's view, President Truman was operating in this third category—in the face of congressional disapproval of his actions.

Jackson's concurrence became the true legacy of the *Youngstown Sheet & Tube* case. To this day, scholars and judges refer to his three-part framework to evaluate fundamental questions about the lawfulness of executive branch actions.

Truman purportedly asked a top adviser to list on a single sheet of paper the reasons why the Court's decision was wrong. The first line of the paper, we're told, read as follows: "The Supreme Court substituted its judgment for that of the President as to the seriousness of the cessation of production of steel at this time."[11] When the President was invited to a dinner with the Justices, he reportedly went to the dinner armed with that list of wrongs.

We will never know for certain whether Truman delivered that message to the Justices. It is rumored, however, that at the close of the dinner, he turned to Justice Black and quipped, "I don't like your law, but this is mighty good bourbon."[12]

MORE RECENT EXAMPLES WHERE the President and Supreme Court have advanced very different perspectives on significant matters

*Chief Justice Rehnquist, Justice O'Connor, Justice Scalia, and John O'Connor
waiting for President George W. Bush's first inauguration in 2001.*

involve the War on Terror, which began in the aftermath of the
September 11, 2001, attacks against the United States. Those attacks on American soil spawned not only fear and terror, but
legislation—both in the United States and abroad—to combat
terrorism and prevent future attacks.

The U.S. Congress adopted the Authorization for the Use of
Military Force (AUMF), which gave President George W. Bush
the authority to use military force against the entities responsible
for the attacks. It also gave the President authority to prevent
future terrorist attacks. Using this law, the President sent U.S.
troops to Afghanistan to wage war against al-Qaeda and the Tal-
iban. The President also set up a detention center at the U.S.
naval base in Guantánamo Bay, Cuba, and established protocols
to try the detainees. These actions prompted several major Supreme Court decisions on the scope of the Executive's power in
prosecuting the War on Terror.

In *Hamdi v. Rumsfeld,* the first of these cases, the Supreme

Court considered the case of Yaser Hamdi, an American-born citizen who was captured on a battlefield in Afghanistan. He was brought back to the United States and designated an "enemy combatant." Hamdi's father filed a lawsuit contending that his son should be permitted to challenge this designation.

In June 2004, the Court, in an opinion I authored, held that "a citizen-detainee seeking to challenge his classification as an enemy combatant must receive notice of the factual basis for his classification, and a fair opportunity to rebut the government's factual assertions before a neutral decisionmaker."[13] The government had argued that the separation of powers required that the courts play a far more limited role in reviewing discretionary judgments of the executive branch. The Court, however, viewed that position as sweeping aside the judiciary's essential role in maintaining the "delicate balance of governance."[14] A "state of war," we concluded, "is not a blank check for the President when it comes to rights of the Nation's citizens."[15]

In *Hamdan v. Rumsfeld,* the Court considered the permissibility of the military tribunals set up by the President to try detainees, and the limited rights available in such proceedings. The Court determined that Congress had authorized the Executive to try suspected terrorists in military tribunals in only exceptional circumstances. However, the Court set the standard procedural rules of courts-martial as the baseline to be used in such trials, rather than the more limited rights the government had provided. While the administration may be permitted to change or adapt those rules, it must demonstrate that using the standard courts-martial rules would be impracticable. Four members of the Court in *Hamdan* also indicated that the proposed military tribunals violated Article 3 of the Geneva Conventions, which requires that criminal sentences be issued by "a regularly constituted court affording all the judicial guarantees recognized as indispensable by civilized peoples."[16]

After the Supreme Court decided *Hamdan,* Congress passed the Military Commissions Act (MCA), which some believed repealed all the federal courts' jurisdiction over the claims of those who have been designated enemy combatants. As a result of the MCA, lower-court habeas corpus challenges filed by prisoners at Guantánamo questioning their detainment were dismissed for lack of jurisdiction.

In *Boumediene v. Bush,* the Supreme Court held that the United States' exercise of authority over Guantánamo gave the detainees a constitutional right to bring their habeas corpus claims in federal district courts. The Court also held that the procedures authorized under the Military Commissions Act, which called for military tribunals to look into the detention of the Guantánamo detainees, were not an adequate substitute for habeas. As the Court explained, "[t]he laws and Constitution are designed to survive, and remain in force, even in extraordinary times. Liberty and security can be reconciled; and in our system, they are reconciled within the framework of the law."[17]

What the War on Terror cases illustrate is the vigorous interchange between our branches of government. The interchange is ongoing, with many difficult questions unanswered. But the courts have played a vibrant role in imposing core principles of liberty upon the critical enterprise of national security. In a sense, democracy has been the fulcrum of the balance; the structure of our government has provided the mechanism of mediation.

WHEN THE FOUNDERS CRAFTED the masterful Constitution that survives to this day, could they have imagined the drama of these stories? Could they have anticipated the human dynamics and battles of will that would pepper the centuries to come and change the course of history in such fascinating ways? Perhaps. Certainly, at a minimum, they foresaw that there would be times of crisis—real and perceived, international and domestic, personal and political—and that these times would inevitably put the President in the boundary-pushing role of defining his own powers, and the courts in the precarious role of reviewing the President's acts. They knew, because common sense dictates as

Cartoon by Guernsey Le Pelley, 1974. It shows President Nixon holding on to audiotapes while being flung off a seesaw marked "Executive Privilege." The catapult is powered by a gavel marked "Supreme Court."

much, that institutions that are large in power and large in their impact inevitably have run-ins that are large in scale and large in their ultimate consequences.

But they also trusted that, in times of trial, their balanced system of government would provide an even larger perspective. They knew that the people of their fledgling nation could be counted on to choose their leaders wisely, and that those chosen could be counted on to respect the roles set forth for them.

As we face the challenges of today, we can find great hope in the dignity with which the presidency and the judiciary have emerged from even the rockiest episodes of the past. No doubt one hundred years from now Americans will recognize that the tasks before this generation were also large. But I believe they will conclude that we, like our forebears, were strong enough to meet them.

THE CALL TO SERVE
Judicial Appointments
———//———

ONE OF THE MORE INTERESTING EVENTS IN OUR NATION'S governance is the selection of a new Justice for the Supreme Court. Our Constitution, in Article II, Section 2, provides that the President has power, with the advice and consent of the Senate, to appoint judges of the Supreme Court.

Every President, except William Henry Harrison, Zachary Taylor, and Jimmy Carter, has had an opportunity to appoint at least one Justice. In 1866, President Andrew Johnson nominated Henry Stanbery to fill a vacancy, but Congress renounced the vacancy by eliminating the seat. President Johnson never got a second chance to fill a Court vacancy. President Washington, on the other hand, nominated eleven Justices. President Andrew Jackson appointed six, including Roger Taney, and Franklin Roosevelt appointed nine, including Robert Jackson.

Every President making appointments has tried to appoint people who were politically acceptable to the President himself. However, a few Presidents later came to regret one or more of their appointments, while others would come to celebrate their appointments as among their proudest achievements.

President Ronald Reagan and Justice Sandra Day O'Connor in 1981.

Take President John Adams. A principal part of Adams's legacy as President was the appointment of John Marshall, who served as Chief Justice for more than thirty-four years. Marshall became known as "the Great Chief Justice." Many of the fundamental legal questions about the Constitution were decided by the so-called Marshall Court. As we have seen, Marshall's opinion in *Marbury v. Madison*[1] established the principle, which was

Portrait of James Madison.

not spelled out expressly in the Constitution, that the Court had the power to determine the constitutionality of laws passed by Congress. His opinion for the Court in *McCulloch v. Maryland*,[2] meanwhile, affirmed the supremacy of the Constitution and made clear that the federal government derives its power directly from the people rather than from the states. President Adams himself once said, "My gift of John Marshall to the people of the United States was the proudest act of my life." Today, a large bronze statue of John Marshall is prominently featured on the ground floor of the Supreme Court as an homage to his important contributions.

Or consider President James Madison, our fourth President, who selected Joseph Story of Massachusetts as his pick for the Court. Story served as a Justice from 1811 to 1845. Though he was only thirty-two when appointed to his seat—making him the youngest Supreme Court Justice in history—Story earned a place alongside Marshall, his colleague and close friend, as one of the greatest Justices of the Court.

Story became a Justice at a time when the American constitutional system was in its infancy, and he was instrumental in establishing a robust role for the federal courts in preserving that system envisioned by the Founding Fathers. Story's influence, moreover, extended to far-reaching areas of the law. He promoted the notion of a uniform commercial system and helped develop admiralty law, patent law, and equity jurisprudence.

Story also left an enormous legacy of constitutional scholarship. His comprehensive treatise on the U.S. Constitution, *Commentaries on the Constitution of the United States,* is one of the seminal sources of historical information on early American jurisprudence and remains a crucial source of historical information on the early days of our constitutional system.

Interestingly, Story, despite his reputation as a brilliant lawyer, had not been President Madison's first choice for Justice. Madison's first choice for a Justice was his own Attorney General,

Levi Lincoln of Massachusetts. Lincoln was sixty-one years old and was losing his eyesight. He informed Madison that he did not want the appointment. President Madison ignored Lincoln's response and made the appointment anyway, but Lincoln refused it. Madison then nominated Alexander Wolcott of Connecticut, but the Senate promptly rejected his nomination. Madison then selected John Quincy Adams, the son of John Adams, but Adams rejected the appointment on the grounds that he had too little legal background and too much political ambition. (In fact, he would later become our sixth President.)

President Madison presumably was then weary of trying to make successful appointments to the Court. He waited seven months before he finally nominated Story. Thomas Jefferson was strongly opposed to Story's appointment, calling him a "pseudo-Republican," a "political chameleon," and an "independent political schemer."[3] Nevertheless, the Senate took only three days to confirm the Story appointment. And with that appointment, they elevated a legal giant who made innumerable contributions to the legal system over his lifetime.

For other early presidents, like President Washington, the appointment process was more of a mixed bag. Washington, as mentioned, sought to appoint men who were strong supporters of the Constitution, were reliable supporters of the Federalist cause, had service in the Revolution, were active in the political life of the nominee's state, and were favorably regarded by the President or other well-known Federalists. But because Washington nominated such prominent statesmen, and the young Supreme Court was not yet the prominent institution that Chief Justice Marshall would make it, few of Washington's nominees stayed for very long.

John Jay, selected by Washington as the Court's first Chief Justice, was a New Yorker and had been influential in obtaining New York's ratification of the Constitution. Despite his judicial office, however, he was sent to England to negotiate what would later be known as the Jay Treaty, which resolved various claims that America and England had against each other as a result of damages incurred during the Revolution. During his absence, Jay's political prominence led him to be nominated and elected governor of New York without so much as a single campaign speech. On his return, he resigned as Chief Justice to assume his elected office; he thought the Supreme Court would never amount to much.

Jay was not the only Washington nominee to prefer other offices over Justice of the Supreme Court. John Rutledge was confirmed by the Senate as an Associate Justice, but despite his confirmation, Rutledge resigned before the Court actually sat in order to become Chief Justice of South Carolina. When John Jay resigned as Chief Justice, President Washington chose Rutledge again, this time to be the new Chief Justice of the United States. Ironically, perhaps, the Senate refused to confirm Rutledge for Jay's seat as Chief Justice in large part because Rutledge had been an outspoken critic of the Jay Treaty.

The other men selected by President Washington for the original six-member Supreme Court were James Wilson of Pennsylvania, John Blair Jr. of Virginia, William Cushing of Massachusetts, and Robert Hanson Harrison of Maryland. Like Rutledge, Robert Harrison resigned soon after his confirmation as an Associate Justice to become chancellor of Maryland, an important judicial post. The last of the original Court members was James Iredell of North Carolina.

The Supreme Court had little to do in its early years. The burden of traveling to and from Court sittings, first in Philadelphia, then in New York City, and finally in Washington, D.C., was substantial. Like Chief Justice Jay, several Justices thought the Court would never be very significant. As a result the tenure of most was relatively brief. Only Justice Cushing stayed for a long time—twenty-one years.

Nevertheless, President Washington did have one of his appointments impeached. When Justice Blair resigned, President Washington selected Samuel Chase of Maryland to fill the vacancy. Chase, thought by many to be outspoken and acid-tongued, made many disparaging comments about Thomas Jefferson and the Republicans after he became a Justice, both before and after Jefferson became President. The House of Representatives impeached Justice Chase during Jefferson's presidency, alleging he had committed "high crimes and misdemeanors." The Senate did not find Chase guilty, by a small margin of four votes, but an important precedent had been established.

President Washington's last appointment to the Court was Oliver Ellsworth of Connecticut, who was nominated and confirmed as Chief Justice after Jay resigned and the Senate rejected Rutledge. Ellsworth served only four years and resigned for ill health.

By the time Thomas Jefferson became President, he felt that he had work to do. All of the Justices were Federalists appointed by Washington and Adams, including Chief Justice John Marshall, whose presence was already being felt. Hoping to balance out their influence, Jefferson made three appointments to the Court, each a "Republican-Democrat." His third appointment resulted from Congress's enlargement of the Court to seven members.

Jefferson instituted a new procedure by asking every member of Congress to suggest the names of two people for consideration for the Supreme Court for the new vacancy. The resulting choices were William Johnson of South Carolina, Henry Brockholst Livingston of New York, and Thomas Todd of Kentucky. Jefferson had hoped that appointing these Republican-Democrats would curb the power of Chief Justice Marshall, but in that effort, he failed. His appointees generally went along with Marshall's opinions. Later, in 1820, when he was out of office, Jefferson described the members of the Supreme Court as a "subtle corps of sappers and miners" consisting of a "crafty chief judge" and "lazy or timid associates."[4]

Other than President Madison's already-mentioned appointment of Justice Story, the next President who had a major influence on the Supreme Court's history was Andrew Jackson. Jackson made six Supreme Court appointments, including John Marshall's successor as Chief Justice, Roger Taney of Maryland. Jackson's Supreme Court selections were largely driven by geography and political loyalty. One of his early appointments was John McLean, who had been postmaster general. While serving on the Court, McLean ran for President four times, each time for a different party and each time unsuccessfully.

Taney was widely regarded as an excellent Chief Justice, although he and the Supreme Court have been criticized for handing down the worst opinion in the Court's history—"the Dred Scott decision" of 1857.[5] The decision ruled that "the negro race" could not be citizens and that slaves were property of their masters. It further held that the Missouri Compromise, an 1820 agreement between proslavery and antislavery factions over the extension of slavery in the Western territories, was unconstitutional. The Dred Scott decision was thought to hasten the Civil War, and it tarred Taney's reputation. Congress refused to apportion the funds for a bust of Taney at the Supreme Court—to join those of the prior Chief Justices—until Taney's successor had died, almost twenty years after Taney's own death.

The worst luck in Supreme Court nominations, however, clearly belongs to the Whig Presidents. General William Henry Harrison, hero of the Battle of Tippecanoe, became our first Whig President in 1841. He was also the first President to make no Supreme Court nomination. It was perhaps his own fault, at least in part—his two-hour inaugural address on a very cold day gave him pneumonia and he died after thirty-one days in office. John Tyler succeeded Harrison and over approximately thirteen months, he made five Supreme Court nominations that failed to be confirmed. He succeeded with only one nomination, of Samuel Nelson of New York, who served almost thirty years.

President James Knox Polk, a Democrat, defeated Henry Clay in 1844 and successfully appointed Levi Woodbury to replace Justice Story and Robert Cooper Grier to replace Justice Henry Baldwin. Polk had twice offered Baldwin's seat to future President James Buchanan, but Buchanan twice refused, perhaps wisely. After Polk's term ended, Zachary Taylor retook the White House for the Whigs, only to become the second President to make no Supreme Court nominations when he died in office in 1850.

President Abraham Lincoln was the next President to have a major impact on the Court, filling five vacancies during his four years in office. His most impressive appointment was Samuel Freeman Miller of Iowa. He had both a medical and a law degree. He had strong support from the North and there was even a petition to Lincoln from 129 of 140 members of the House of Representatives urging selection of Miller for the Court. Presi-

Chief Justice Roger B. Taney administering the oath of office to Abraham Lincoln in 1861.

dent Lincoln was pleased to make the nomination and the Senate confirmed it unanimously and immediately. Miller more than justified the confidence shown in his selection. Another noteworthy appointee by Lincoln was Stephen J. Field of California, a strong property rights advocate who is discussed in depth later in this book (see Larger-Than-Life Justices).

Chief Justice Taney died in 1864. The selection of a replacement as Chief Justice was challenging for Lincoln. He ultimately selected Samuel Chase, who had run against Lincoln for the presidency and continued to have political ambitions. Chase's nomination was promptly confirmed, eliminating one of Lincoln's political rivals, but giving the country one of its more distinguished Chief Justices. Indeed, when Lincoln's successor, Andrew Johnson, was impeached by the House and tried by the Senate as a result of political fissures in the wake of the Civil War, Chief Justice Chase skillfully presided over the impeachment trial. In the end, the Senate vote was only one short of convicting Johnson.

For the remainder of the nineteenth century, few if any Supreme Court nominations or nominees would prove worthy of an important place in American history textbooks, with the lone exception of John Marshall Harlan of Kentucky. Named for the great Chief Justice, Harlan was nominated by President Rutherford B. Hayes and served thirty-four years. He distinguished himself on the Supreme Court as "the Great Dissenter," issuing solo dissents from the Court's majority in two of the most critical cases of his tenure. In 1883, he authored a strident dissenting opinion in the *Civil Rights Cases*, which held that federal civil rights legislation enacted in the wake of the Civil War was unconstitutional. And in 1896, Harlan was the lone dissenter in *Plessy v. Ferguson*, which upheld the old doctrine of "separate but equal" that allowed racial segregation in public schools and facilities. Harlan famously wrote: "Our Constitution is color-blind and neither knows nor tolerates classes among citizens. In respect of civil rights, all citizens are equal before the law." Those words would be proven right when *Plessy* was overruled by *Brown v. Board of Education* more than forty years after Harlan's death.

The next nominations of note belonged to President Theodore Roosevelt, who succeeded to the presidency in 1901 when President William McKinley died in office. President Roosevelt

Chief Justice William Howard Taft, circa 1920s.

wrote: "I should hold myself as guilty of an irreparable wrong to the nation if I should put [on the Court] any man who was not absolutely sane and sound on the great national policies for which we stand in public life."[6] Roosevelt considered geographic origins unimportant. He made three appointments: Oliver Wendell Holmes Jr., William H. Moody, and William R. Day.

Holmes, discussed further in Larger-Than-Life Justices, is consistently ranked as one of our country's great Justices. Suffice it to say here that he did not confuse constitutionality with wisdom. He said that "when the people . . . want to do something that I can't find anything in the Constitution expressly forbidding them to do, I say, whether I like it or not, 'Goddamit, let 'em do it.' "[7]

William Howard Taft, a Roosevelt protégé who succeeded Roosevelt as President, was able to appoint five Justices and elevate another to Chief Justice during his single four-year term. Taft chose his appointees with great care, based on intellect and judicial experience. He chose Horace H. Lurton, a professor at Vanderbilt Law School and judge on the U.S. Court of Appeals for the Sixth Circuit, and then Charles Evans Hughes, governor of New York. Lurton's appointment surprised some observers because he was a Democrat. Soon after, Chief Justice Melville Fuller died and Taft had that position to fill. He had indicated to Hughes in a letter that he would consider appointing Hughes as Chief Justice if it became vacant. After waiting over six months, Taft finally nominated Justice Edward Douglas White as Chief Justice. In making that appointment, Taft let it be known that "there is nothing I would have loved more than being Chief Justice of the United States. I cannot help seeing the irony in the fact that I, who desire that office so much, should now be signing the commission of another man."[8]

Taft also appointed Willis Van Devanter of Wyoming, who was a judge on the Eighth Circuit, and Joseph Rucker Lamar of Georgia, who had once served on the Georgia Supreme Court.

His final appointment was that of Mahlon Pitney, a former New Jersey congressman and judge.

In 1912, President Taft failed to win reelection. His successor, Woodrow Wilson, served eight years. He made three appointments to the Court: Louis D. Brandeis, John H. Clarke, and James C. McReynolds.

There is an irony in two of these appointments. Justice Louis Brandeis was the first Jewish Justice of the Supreme Court, and—with Justice Holmes—would distinguish himself as one of the great Justices and legal minds of his generation. Justice James McReynolds, on the other hand, would distinguish himself as a notorious racist, and he infamously refused even to speak to Justice Brandeis (and later, Justice Benjamin Cardozo, appointed by President Hoover) because of his anti-Semitism. He was a very disagreeable member of the Court and is poorly regarded to this day. He, too, is discussed later in this book.

Justice Brandeis's nomination resulted in substantial opposition; he was known as "the People's Lawyer" and his detractors described him as a radical, anticorporate crusader for social justice who lacked a judicial temperament. Nonetheless, Brandeis was eventually confirmed by a vote of 47 to 22, and served with distinction.

Warren G. Harding became President after Wilson, and former President Taft got his wish. Although Harding died in office after only two and a half years, he appointed four people to the Court, including Taft as Chief Justice, the position Taft had wanted above all others. Harding's other appointments to the Court were George Sutherland, Edward T. Sanford, and Pierce Butler.

Taft was elated with his elevation to Chief Justice. He worked exceedingly hard on the Court, writing about 20 percent of all the opinions, persuading Congress to build a Supreme Court building, and coordinating the federal courts. Taft served nine effective years before he died in 1930.

President Calvin "Silent Cal" Coolidge succeeded Harding. The Coolidge campaign slogan was "The business of the United States is business." It did not, however, include much work with the Supreme Court. President Coolidge appointed only one Justice, his Attorney General, Harlan Fiske Stone of New Hampshire. When Stone's nomination drew some Senate criticism, he became the first Court nominee to appear in person before the Senate Judiciary Committee, where he responded exceedingly well to the questions and was easily confirmed. He proved to be very independent as an Associate Justice and often joined the dissenters, Holmes and Brandeis. Stone was eventually made Chief Justice by Franklin Delano Roosevelt.

President Coolidge was succeeded by President Herbert Hoover, another Republican. Although Hoover's presidency was saddled by the stock market crash of 1929 and the Great Depression, he nominated three impressive Justices: Charles Evans Hughes as Chief Justice to succeed the terminally ill Chief Justice Taft, and Benjamin Cardozo and Owen J. Roberts as Associate Justices. He had nominated John J. Parker for Associate Justice but Parker was rejected by a narrow margin.

The Cardozo nomination was made on the retirement of Oliver Wendell Holmes. Cardozo was considered a liberal. He was strongly supported by the entire law school faculty of the University of Chicago and by the law school deans of Harvard, Yale, and Columbia, as well as powerful Senate Foreign Relations Committee chair William Borah. It was Justice Cardozo who authored the significant opinion for the Court in *Palko v. Connecticut*.[9] That opinion clarified that the Due Process Clause of the Constitution protects only those rights that are "of the very essence of a scheme of ordered liberty" and held that the Court should therefore gradually apply portions of the Bill of Rights to the states, not just to the federal government.

Franklin Roosevelt, who succeeded Coolidge, served as President from 1933 to 1945, an unprecedented length of time that, of course, includes most of the Great Depression and World War II. He made nine nominations, second only to George Washington, and he left a lasting impact on the Court.

During Roosevelt's first term as President, a majority of the Supreme Court found a number of his New Deal laws unconstitutional. As mentioned earlier, Roosevelt was so disturbed by the Court's actions that he sent to Congress a proposed bill that would give the President authority to appoint an additional Justice, up to a maximum of six, for every sitting member of the Court over the age of seventy. It would have allowed the Supreme Court to increase from nine to fifteen Justices.

The President's arguments about the Supreme Court were disingenuous at best. He claimed the Court was overworked and that the Justices were physically incapable of doing their work. These claims were easily refuted. The Court was demonstrably up to date with its docket. Many lawyers and academics opposed the bill and it was defeated.

Perhaps also contributing to its defeat was the so-called "switch in time that saved nine." In a 1937 case, *West Coast Hotel Co. v. Parrish*,[10] Justice Owen Roberts unexpectedly voted with Chief Justice Hughes and Justices Brandeis, Cardozo, and Stone to uphold a state minimum wage law. Many commentators regarded Roberts's vote as a sudden and calculated maneuver to thwart the pending court-packing plan.

In addition, Justice Van Devanter decided to retire, which gave President Roosevelt his first Court appointment, that of Senator Hugo Black of Alabama. His other eight nominations were Stanley F. Reed, Felix Frankfurter, William O. Douglas, Frank Murphy, James F. Byrnes, Robert Jackson, Wiley Rutledge, and the elevation of Justice Harlan F. Stone to Chief Justice.

It was an entirely new Court. President Roosevelt sought assurance that judicial nominees would be loyal to his New Deal principles, libertarian in outlook, and supportive of his wartime aims. In all of that he succeeded. The Court met President Roosevelt's expectations.

On April 12, 1945, First Lady Eleanor Roosevelt told Vice President Harry Truman that her husband had passed away. Although Truman was surprised to be taking over as President, he himself surprised many Americans by becoming a strong and impressive leader. When he had opportunities to appoint Justices to the Court he selected in each instance men who were his friends. There were four appointees: Harold H. Burton, a former U.S. Senate colleague; Fred Vinson, secretary of the Treasury; Tom C. Clark, the U.S. Attorney General; and Sherman Minton, fellow former senator. Vinson had held several government posts under Roosevelt and served as a member of Congress. When Chief Justice Stone died suddenly in 1946, President Truman selected Fred Vinson as the new Chief Justice. He served, rather unhappily, for about seven years. Reportedly, the Court at the time was racked by infighting, and Vinson found himself a poor fit for leadership.

Truman's friendship with his nominees did not help him much in the most important case of his tenure as President. He was greatly disappointed when a majority of the Court, including Justice Clark, held that the President's seizure of the steel mills during the Korean War was unconstitutional.

Dwight David Eisenhower was elected President on the Republican ticket in 1952. A popular president, he was reelected and made five appointments to the Court during his two terms. His first was the selection of a Chief Justice after Vinson died in September 1953. Earl Warren was governor of California, having served as an attorney and a public prosecutor before being elected to that position. He was confirmed as Chief Justice unanimously.

Warren had a great impact on the Court. In 1954, the Supreme Court decided *Brown v. Board of Education*,[11] vindicating Harlan's dissent in *Plessy v. Ferguson* and declaring a legal end to separate public schools for black and white students. It is said that Warren's leadership contributed to the unanimity of the opinion in *Brown,* which proved important in the acceptance of that historic decision. President Eisenhower deserves some credit as well: There was considerable opposition to the efforts of the lower federal courts to implement *Brown,* and although President Eisenhower was probably not among its enthusiastic supporters, to his credit, in September 1957 he sent federal troops to Little Rock, Arkansas, to enforce the decision and enable African American students to enter the public schools in the face of Governor Orval Faubus's strenuous efforts to prevent it.

Several other important cases were decided during Chief Justice Warren's tenure. One was *Reynolds v. Simms,*[12] which applied the principle of "one person, one vote" to state legislative districts. Another significant decision during Chief Justice Warren's tenure was *Miranda v. Arizona,*[13] which famously required that criminal defendants in custody be advised of their right to consult with an attorney and of other legal rights prior to being questioned.

When Justice Robert Jackson died in 1954, President Eisenhower appointed John Marshall Harlan II of New York, the grandson of the first Justice John Marshall Harlan. The third appointee was a Democrat from the New Jersey Supreme Court, William J. Brennan Jr.

Sometime later President Eisenhower was reportedly asked by a biographer if he had made any mistakes as President. He said, "Yes, two, and they are both sitting on the Supreme Court."[14] He was referring to Chief Justice Warren and Justice Brennan— both of whom proved far more liberal than he had anticipated.

President Eisenhower's fourth appointment to the Court was that of Charles Evans Whittaker of Missouri, made upon the retirement of Stanley Reed. Eisenhower's fifth and last appointment was Potter Stewart of Ohio, who had been serving on the U.S. Court of Appeals for the Sixth Circuit.

During his brief term in office John F. Kennedy made two appointments to the Court: Byron R. White and Arthur J. Goldberg. They had both helped in his election campaign and the President knew them well. Byron White is notable as a true scholar athlete. He grew up in a small town in Colorado, worked in the fields and on a railroad, earned a Phi Beta Kappa key at the University of Colorado, and was an all-American football player. He played professional football for the Pittsburgh Steelers and later the Detroit Lions, and was a Rhodes Scholar. Like Kennedy, he had served in the navy as well. He was a very capable and independent Justice on the Court, and a wonderful colleague of mine, until his retirement in 1993.

Lyndon Johnson, who of course succeeded President Kennedy after Kennedy's assassination in 1963, made four nominations to the Court, but succeeded with only two. The first was Abe Fortas, who was appointed after President Johnson persuaded Arthur Goldberg to retire from the Court to serve as ambassador to the United Nations. Fortas had helped Johnson as a lawyer as far back as seventeen years earlier in a very close Senate contest in Texas. Fortas served on the Court for four years.

In 1968, when Chief Justice Warren revealed his plans to retire, Johnson announced his intention to nominate Abe Fortas as Chief Justice and William Homer Thornberry for the Associate Justice position. The timing of all these announcements was unfortunate. After various disclosures of certain earnings of Abe Fortas and resulting negative press, Justice Fortas asked the President to withdraw his nomination as Chief Justice. Earl Warren remained as Chief Justice for another year, during which period Fortas made further financial disclosures. Fortas ultimately resigned from the Court.

In the meantime, Justice Tom Clark announced his retirement and President Johnson nominated Thurgood Marshall to be Clark's replacement. Marshall would be the first African American to serve on the Court. President Johnson announced that the nomination was "the right thing to do, the right time to do it, the right man and the right place."[15] Marshall was best known for his work as chief counsel of the National Association for the Advancement of Colored People, in which role he successfully argued many civil rights cases in the Supreme Court, including *Brown v. Board of Education*.[16] At the time of his nomination, Marshall was serving as President Johnson's Solicitor General, representing the United States in litigation before the Supreme Court. Marshall was ultimately confirmed by the Senate by a vote of 69 to 11.

Richard Nixon took office in 1969 and appointed a total of four Supreme Court Justices: Warren Burger, Harry Blackmun, Lewis Powell, and William Rehnquist. All four were future colleagues of mine. Burger was the first in line. Then a judge on the U.S. Court of Appeals for the D.C. Circuit, Burger was appointed as Chief Justice in 1969 to replace Chief Justice Warren. Blackmun was nominated the following year and was confirmed unanimously. Blackmun was a longtime friend of Burger; in fact, Burger had been Blackmun's best man and had recommended him to fill the vacancy. In 1972, Powell and Rehnquist took their seats on the bench. President Nixon had nominated the two men on the same day—Powell, to replace Justice Black, and Rehnquist, to replace Justice Harlan. Powell, reluctant to leave private practice, had actually refused President Nixon's request that he join the Court in 1969, but he was persuaded the second time around by the President and his Attorney General. Rehnquist had been working for the Nixon administration, heading the Office of Legal Counsel at the Justice Department. In 1986, he would be elevated to Chief Justice.

After Nixon's resignation in 1974, Gerald Ford became President. Ford made just one appointment to the Supreme Court, John Paul Stevens in 1975. Justice Stevens, who had been serving on the U.S. Court of Appeals for the Seventh Circuit, sailed through the confirmation process. The Senate confirmed him unanimously. Interestingly, Stevens replaced the longest-serving

JUSTICE SANDRA O'CONNOR   10-5-81

*Cartoon by Taylor Jones showing Justice O'Connor
and the Reverend Jerry Falwell.*

Justice in the Court's history, Justice Douglas, and went on to become the third-longest-serving Justice himself, with nearly thirty-five years on the Supreme Court bench.

My own nomination followed. President Ronald Reagan took office in January 1981. During his presidential campaign, Reagan had pledged to appoint the first woman to the Court and he soon got his chance when Justice Stewart announced his retirement. As the first female nominee for the position of Associate Justice, I was under an unrelenting media spotlight during my confirmation process. But I was confirmed unanimously by the Senate in September 1981 and went on to serve on the Court for the next twenty-five years.

President Reagan also appointed Antonin Scalia and Anthony Kennedy as Associate Justices, in 1986 and 1988, respectively. Both continue to sit on the Court. Indeed, of the ten Justices who have been appointed since my own confirmation, only Justice David Souter, who was appointed by President George H. W. Bush in 1990, and I have retired.

The others all remain active. Clarence Thomas, appointed in 1991 by President George H. W. Bush, replaced Justice Marshall. Ruth Bader Ginsburg and Stephen Breyer, appointed by President Bill Clinton in 1993 and 1994, respectively, replaced Justice White and Justice Blackmun. Both Justice Thomas and Justice Ginsburg were, at the time of their nominations, federal judges on the U.S. Court of Appeals for the District of Columbia Circuit. Justice Breyer, meanwhile, had been Chief Judge of the First Circuit and based in Boston, Massachusetts.

What followed was a remarkable eleven-year stretch during which there were no changes of personnel on the Court. Justice Breyer remained the junior justice for those eleven years. In 2005, however, the nation saw a rapid succession of new vacancies and nominations to the Court. President George W. Bush appointed John G. Roberts and Samuel Alito to serve as Chief Justice and Associate Justice, in 2005 and 2006, respectively, filling the vacancies left by Rehnquist and myself. Harriet Miers, a Texan woman then serving as the White House Counsel, was initially nominated to the position that Justice Alito would eventually fill. President Bush, however, withdrew Miers's nomination at her request before the Senate Judiciary Committee even began deliberating.

Most recently, President Barack Obama appointed two more female Justices, Sonia Sotomayor and Elena Kagan, in 2009 and 2010, respectively, following the retirements of Souter and Stevens.

As of this writing, there have been 112 Justices who were confirmed and actually served on the Court. By contrast, 27 Supreme Court nominations have failed. Of those 27, the Senate formally rejected 11, postponed 3, tabled 5, and took no action in 4. The remaining 4 nominations were withdrawn by the President.[17]

There are no legal or constitutional requirements for a federal judge or justice, although today it would be highly unlikely that a President would nominate a federal jurist who had no law degree and no experience as a lawyer or judge. The last Justices of the Supreme Court who did not have a law degree were Justice Robert Jackson and Justice Stanley Reed, both appointed by President Franklin Roosevelt.

Indeed, the current norm is to appoint individuals who have previous experience as federal judges. Although a majority of the Justices through the Court's history had no prior judicial experience, eight of the nine current members have previously served as judges on a federal court of appeals. Prior to Justice Kagan's recent appointment, I was the last Justice not to come from a federal court of appeals, although Justice Souter served only briefly on the First Circuit before his elevation to the Supreme Court. I had served as a state court judge in Arizona prior to my appointment; Justice Kagan had served most recently as dean of Harvard Law School and U.S. Solicitor General before becoming Associate Justice of the Supreme Court.

New Justices come and go, but the judicial appointment process has become a fixture of our nation's governance. Whether on the outside or the inside, it is always fascinating to see how the selection of the nine members of the Court contributes to and shapes the development of the law.

A HOUSE IS NOT A HOME

The Journey to One First Street

———//———

ON FRIDAY, SEPTEMBER 25, 1981, THE DAY OF MY INVESTI-
ture as a Supreme Court Justice, I walked out of the
Court and descended the wide marble steps with Chief
Justice Warren Burger for the first time. Those grandly propor-
tioned bronze doors and marble stairway are the iconic images of
the Supreme Court. They have graced many a postcard and
book cover. Yet many people do not realize that it took 145 years
for the Supreme Court to get there. During those years the Court
was a virtual nomad, having several different homes before finally ending up at One First Street, in our nation's capital.

In fact, the first sessions of the Supreme Court were not in
Washington, D.C., at all. They were in New York. The Merchants
Exchange Building, in what is now the financial district of New
York City, was the site of the very first courtroom of the Supreme
Court. After John Jay took the oath as the first Chief Justice on
October 19, 1789, he called the Court to assemble in the Ex-
change Building on February 1, 1790. The Exchange, located at
the intersection of Broad and Water streets, was a brick building
owned by the city of New York.[1] The space upstairs was occupied

The Old Royal Exchange Building, circa late 1700s.

by tenants who maintained a "coffee-room," sold imported goods, and conducted exhibitions and meetings.[2]

The Court's early sessions in the Exchange were brief and uneventful. The Justices did not have any cases on their docket. Indeed, not a single case was filed in the year 1790, though the number climbed to a remarkable two in 1791 and five in 1792.[3] Instead, the sessions were devoted to selecting officers of the Court, settling on the official seals of the Court and the Courts of Appeals, passing rules, and admitting members to the bar.[4] Justice Rutledge did not even attend the first few sessions.[5]

The lack of a significant workload was probably for the best. It must have been hard to get much accomplished while the Court had no permanent home. No one had thought to build the Supreme Court a permanent physical structure, most likely because no one knew for sure at the time what would become of this institution.

* * *

THINGS STARTED LOOKING UP when in that year, 1792, Congress passed the Residence Act, which identified a district on the Potomac River "not exceeding ten miles square" as the permanent seat of the federal government starting in 1800, and designated Philadelphia as the interim capital.[6] When Philadelphia became the seat of government from December 1790, the Court moved there, too.

The Court's second home became Independence Hall in Philadelphia, then known as the State House. Independence Hall, located on Chestnut Street between Fifth and Sixth Streets, was where the Declaration of Independence and the United States Constitution were debated and adopted. For the February 1791 Term, the Court met for only two days. A group of Philadelphia lawyers escorted Chief Justice Jay and Justices William Cushing, James Wilson, and James Iredell to the State House to take their seats on the bench in a room on the first floor.[7]

The accommodations were an improvement, but far from

The former Supreme Court Room in Independence Hall.

The Pennsylvania State House (Independence Hall), circa 1898.

ideal. The courtroom was just a forty-foot square featuring three large windows, and it was unheated.[8] The Justices also had some "roommates"—they shared space with the state supreme court and the federal circuit court. To say that quarters were tight is an understatement. The Pennsylvania House of Representatives met right across the hallway. The United States Congress convened a mere hundred feet away. President Washington, meanwhile, lived one block away, a short distance off Sixth Street.[9]

In August 1791, the Court moved to a space on the first floor of the newly constructed City Hall, at the northeast corner of the State House Square. Although the Justices met for just three days that August, they ended up staying at City Hall for nine years.[10] The Court again shared the room, this time with the mayor's court. When the work of the two courts overlapped, it was reportedly the Supreme Court that had to find an alternative venue!

* * *

THE COURT ONCE AGAIN found itself homeless when the capital finally moved to Washington, D.C., in 1800. Congress lent the Supreme Court space in the new Capitol Building, as part of what was expected to be a temporary arrangement. The Justices initially convened in a committee room in the Capitol. After the British set fire to the Capitol in the War of 1812, the Court relocated briefly to a private home.

The Court later returned to the Capitol Building and, from 1819 until 1860, settled in what is now known as the Old Supreme Court Chamber. From that chamber, the Justices issued such landmark decisions as *Gibbons v. Ogden,* which held that the Commerce Clause of the Constitution confers on Congress a broad power to regulate interstate commerce, and the infamous *Dred Scott v. Sandford,* which ruled that slaves were not citizens and not protected by the Constitution.

In 1860, the Court moved upstairs into a chamber that had

The Old Supreme Court Chamber in the U.S. Capitol.

been vacated by the Senate. Designed by architect Benjamin Latrobe, the semicircular, two-story chamber featured an umbrella vault ceiling. This was the Court's home until 1935. The Justices, however, were still dependent on the Senate for library and office space and many of them continued to maintain offices at home, where their clerks and secretaries worked.[11]

IT WAS CHIEF JUSTICE William Howard Taft who, in 1925, formed the vision for the current Supreme Court Building. Taft wished for an edifice that would serve as a testament to the judiciary's dignity and independence as a separate and coequal branch. With his executive experience as President and his connections, he succeeded in lobbying Congress to pass an act in 1928 providing for a Supreme Court Building Commission, and in getting himself appointed to chair it. Taft commissioned his friend, renowned architect Cass Gilbert, for the job. Gilbert had attained prominence earlier in his career with the design of Minnesota's state capitol in 1898, called "the most influential model of neoclassicism among capitols built after the Civil War."[12] The Supreme Court Building was Gilbert's last great commission. On the day he got the job, Gilbert wrote in his journal: "Thus opens a new chapter in my career and at 70 years of age I am now to undertake to carry through the most important and notable work of my life."

Gilbert's task was certainly not an easy one. There was some debate over where the Court should be located. President Herbert Hoover wished to have the building overlooking the Potomac River. Others suggested the current site of the Jefferson Memorial. But Chief Justice Taft persuaded Gilbert that a location closer to the main government offices would be most convenient. The Court was to be wedged on an irregular plot of land adjacent to both the Capitol and the Library of Congress. Lore has it that Gilbert asked where he would find the grassy hill on which he was to build the structure, only to be instructed to fit the structure in across the street.[13]

The architectural dominance of the Capitol and Library of Congress posed a design conundrum. Gilbert was particularly concerned that the dome on the Library of Congress would interfere with the line of sight from the Court building. On one occasion, Gilbert reportedly suggested to Chief Justice Taft that the dome of the Library of Congress be removed![14]

To assert the Court's presence, meanwhile, Gilbert designed an impressive, grand entrance. Thus Gilbert conceived of a plaza leading to forty-four marble steps and a main entrance framed by a double row of sixteen white marble, Corinthian columns.[15] Above the 1,300-pound bronze doors is the inscription EQUAL JUSTICE UNDER LAW. The steps and inscription are intended to inspire visitors and Justices alike. On his nomination to the Supreme Court in 2005, Chief Justice John G. Roberts Jr. confessed, "I always got a lump in my throat whenever I walked up those marble steps to argue a case before the court, and I don't think it was just from the nerves."[16]

Gilbert chose American materials for the construction but made an exception for the courtroom. Yet even the imported materials were finished in the United States. Vermont white marble formed the building's exterior; Georgian and Alabaman marble were used in the main hall and courtyards. The wood in the offices was American quartered white oak. For the main chamber, meanwhile, Gilbert opted for veined Spanish ivory marble for the walls and a yellow and ivory marble for the columns.[17] The new courtroom had 60 percent more floor area and 10 percent more seating than the Court's chamber at the Capitol.[18] It was flanked by twenty-four Ionic columns. At Chief Justice Taft's insistence, Gilbert provided space for the press in front of the bench.[19]

Sadly, Chief Justice Taft did not live to see work begin in 1931 on the building. He died in March 1930, five weeks after his retirement. At a ceremony in 1932, however, Taft's successor as Chief Justice, Charles Evan Hughes, helped President Hoover lay the building's cornerstone.[20] Hughes deemed the new structure a testament to "permanence, not the permanence of stone and steel" but "to an imperishable ideal of liberty under law."[21] The construction costs totaled approximately $9 million.[22]

The Court's permanent home opened in the midst of the Great Depression in 1935. It garnered a mixed critical reception. Gilbert had conceived of his design as a "reaction against the silly modernist movement."[23] But Gilbert's fellow architects deemed the building lacking in imagination, even if stylistically correct. Justice Louis Brandeis was said to have "detested the building" for its monumental pretensions.[24] One of Brandeis's law clerks reported that the Justice "hated everything 'Roman' about Washington."[25]

The Court formally opened the October Term of 1935 in its new home. According to newspaper articles on October 7, 1935, Chief Justice Hughes uttered the first words in the courtroom: "Are there any admissions?"

Fifty years later, I sat in that very courtroom as an Associate Justice of the Supreme Court. We commemorated the anniversary of the building's opening. With Chief Justice Burger presiding, we held a special session in which former Solicitor General Erwin Griswold, Attorney General Edwin Meese, and the president of the American Bar Association, William Falsgraf, offered reflections on the Court's journey over the last half century.[26]

IN MAY 2010, SECURITY concerns led the Court to close the iconic front entrance to the public. Members of the public now enter the building through a security checkpoint on the plaza level. My colleagues, Justice Stephen Breyer and Justice Ruth Bader Ginsburg, issued a dissenting statement from that decision. The main entrance and front steps, they wrote, are "not only a means to,

General view of the west façade of the Supreme Court Building.

but also a metaphor for, access to the court itself."[27] They expressed "hope that the public will one day in the future be able to enter the Court's Great Hall after passing under the famous words, 'Equal Justice Under Law.' " I often think back to my first day walking down those marble steps, which Gilbert imbued with such grace and dignity, and hope the same. But whether seen up close or from afar, the structure of the Supreme Court at One First Street stands as a remarkable symbol of the institution's endurance and journey from humble beginnings.

HUMBLE BEGINNINGS

The First Decade of the United States Supreme Court

———— //————

ANYONE WHO SEES THE SUPREME COURT TODAY IN ALL ITS grandeur would be amazed to know its humble beginnings. The early years of the Court were a tumultuous struggle. It had no home, little money, and virtually no cases; it is a wonder it survived at all! Those humble beginnings, and how they were overcome, have helped shape our democracy.

Article III of the Constitution established the Supreme Court, vesting the "judicial Power of the United States" in "one Supreme Court, and in such inferior Courts as the Congress may from time to time ordain and establish."[1] Congress had to flesh out the rest from these few words.

The Judiciary Act of 1789 set the number of Justices at six.[2] President Washington nominated John Jay of New York to be the Chief Justice[3] and selected five Associate Justices: John Rutledge of South Carolina,[4] James Wilson of Pennsylvania, William Cushing of Massachusetts,[5] Robert H. Harrison of Maryland,[6] and John Blair of Virginia.[7] The six nominees were approved by the Senate just two days later.[8] So far, so good. The initially smooth progress, however, proved short-lived. In a sign of what was to come, Justice Harrison resigned for health reasons before the first session even took place![9] Justice Iredell filled the vacancy left by Justice Harrison.[10]

The Court was up and running, but it had very little to do. Congress provided that the Court would sit in session twice each year, with one session "commencing the first Monday of February, and the other the first Monday of August."[11] The first four Terms, from February 1790 to August 1791, were uneventful. No cases were argued during those Terms and the Justices merely convened for a few days to swear in clerks and lawyers. Justice Rutledge did not even attend for the first few Terms; although he arrived in New York in August 1790 intending to attend the Court meeting, he was incapacitated by gout.[12]

The Court had no stable membership. Chief Justice John Jay resigned in 1795, after just six years of serving as the first Chief. Jay had two reasons for stepping down. First, he had had enough of "circuit-riding," the early practice by which Supreme Court Justices were required by law to travel thousands of miles to serve on lower courts across the country. Second, Jay had learned, upon returning from his extended diplomatic trip to England, that his friends had nominated him to the governorship of New York and obtained his election.[13]

After Jay resigned, President Washington then nominated Rutledge again to replace him.[14] John Rutledge had been one of President Washington's original six Justices, but frustrated by circuit-riding, the lack of activity on the Supreme Court, and being passed over for Chief Justice in favor of Jay, Rutledge had left the court in 1791 to become Chief Justice of the South Carolina Court of Common Pleas.[15]

Rutledge's second confirmation as Chief Justice did not go well. Rutledge was outspoken, perhaps too much so. In July 1795, probably before he received word of his appointment as Chief Justice, he attended a meeting in Charleston and joined other South Carolinians in attacking the Jay Treaty with Great Britain, which ensured, among other things, the withdrawal of the British Army from areas in the Northwest. He believed it was too generous to the British, and he delivered a vehement speech in opposition, reportedly stating that he "had rather the President should die than sign that puerile instrument" and that he "preferred war" to the treaty's adoption.[16] This caused treaty supporters to rally against his nomination.[17] President Washington kept his word, however, and instructed the secretary of state to issue the commission. But this was a recess appointment; the Senate still had to approve Rutledge when it convened again in December. In December 1795, after much heated political debate and the spreading of rumors that Rutledge was insane, the Senate defeated Rutledge's nomination by a vote of 14 to 10.[18] This marked the first time that the Senate rejected a President's recess appointment.

After Rutledge's rejection by the Senate, President Washington nominated sitting Justice William Cushing to fill the Chief Justice's slot, in January 1796.[19] Cushing was quickly confirmed as the Chief.[20] His frail health, however, forced him to return the commission to the President a mere week later.[21] The President next turned to Oliver Ellsworth, who was confirmed in March of that year.[22] Ellsworth's tenure was also short-lived. Less than four years into his tenure, Ellsworth was dispatched as a commissioner to France to renegotiate a treaty on behalf of the United States.[23]

In 1800, President John Adams nominated John Jay to return to the Court, and the Senate confirmed him. But it soon turned out that Jay himself didn't want the job back.[24] Jay declined the post, citing the Court's lack of "energy, weight, and dignity" and his own health problems. Finally, in 1801, his last months in office, Adams nominated John Marshall as Chief Justice. Marshall was unanimously confirmed and served on the Court for thirty-four history-making years.

Getting Justices to stay put was not the only problem the early

Court faced. Early Court records were rife with textual errors, corrections, and revisions. The second Clerk of the Court, Samuel Bayard, did his best to keep drafts of orders and motions, as well as rough minutes, and to maintain a docket book.[25] But Bayard was not even required to reside in the capital. When Washington selected him to prosecute admiralty claims on behalf of the United States in London, off he went for nearly five years. From November 1794 until spring 1798, then, the Justices were without a Clerk of Court.[26]

As for Court Reporters, written opinions were not even required until 1834, during President Andrew Jackson's administration and while Marshall was still Chief Justice.[27] In 1791, when the Court moved from New York to Philadelphia, Alexander James Dallas, a local lawyer, simply showed up one day and appointed himself the first Supreme Court Reporter. Dallas reported cases for personal gain and professional reputation. Indeed, Dallas founded the enterprise of Supreme Court reports almost inadvertently. His main interest lay with state decisions; his first volume was titled *Report of Cases Ruled and Adjudged in the Courts of Pennsylvania, Before and Since the Revolution.* Pennsylvania cases made up his entire first volume of published reports and over half his second. It was only in his second volume that he began adding the opinions of the Supreme Court, which was by then sitting in Philadelphia. In the English tradition, Dallas arranged for publication of the reports and made his money by selling the publications to the public.[28]

Dallas's efforts were admirable, but there were nonetheless serious flaws in his reporting. The lack of institutional precedent no doubt contributed to the uneven quality of the reports. Between 1790 and 1800, a number of important cases went unreported.[29] He reported decisions in only about sixty cases.[30] Some historians believe Dallas failed to report as many as one-third of the decisions rendered during the first decade of the Court. He was also extremely slow. His last volume didn't appear until 1807, seven years after his tenure as Reporter ended.[31] On top of that, his reports contained many inaccuracies.[32] In fairness, however, Dallas doesn't deserve all the blame for these shortcomings. The Justices were partially responsible for the gaps in his reports, because they failed to submit written opinions in most cases.[33]

Dallas's successor, William Cranch, had a somewhat smoother ride. In 1802, Cranch undertook to report and publish the Supreme Court decisions from 1801 to 1815. Cranch reportedly stated that he was "rescued from much anxiety as well as responsibility by the practice which the court had adapted of reducing their opinions to writing in all cases of difficulty or importance."[34] Cranch simultaneously served as a judge on the District of Columbia Circuit Court, however, and in 1817, his judicial duties finally led him to resign as Supreme Court Reporter.

It was in 1817 that the office of the Reporter finally became official. Congress authorized the Court to appoint a salaried Reporter. His name was Henry Wheaton, and his salary was one thousand dollars a year.[35]

HOW DIFFERENT THINGS ARE today. We expect the Justices to serve for decades on the Court. Justices don't have to worry about traveling on horseback through life-threatening floods and ice storms to get to work each day. The Court now occupies one of the most impressive buildings in Washington. The Clerk's and Reporter's offices run like well-oiled machines. This is good not only for the Justices, but also for our democracy.

As the history of the Court—especially of its first decade—demonstrates, it was not always this way. One would not envy the judiciary in those early days, when the Supreme Court Justices barely had any cases and were forced to ride circuit and to hold court in a succession of temporary quarters without a well-organized clerical staff or regular court Reporters. We owe a great deal to the long-suffering souls who laid the foundation for the venerable institution we have today.

In our common-law system, where the law is expounded through case-by-case adjudication, it is essential to have competent Reporters. As Roscoe Pound said: "Ours is a technique of utilizing recorded judicial experience. . . . Even when we have written texts, as on American constitutional law, we proceed at once to look at them through the spectacles of the common law, and our method is not one of development of the text but of development of judicially found grounds of decision which, if they began in the text, have since led an independent existence."[36]

It helps to have an atmosphere that attracts the best and brightest among our highly educated class of professional lawyers—this means, among other things, salaries that cannot be reduced, and, yes, a permanent building. It helps to have people who are well trained and who are willing to spend years in the same line of work, thinking about the same sorts of questions until they get really good at answering them in an atmosphere insulated, as far as possible, from political pressures. I was a Justice for over a quarter of a century, and after hearing a few thousand cases, I think I began to get the hang of it. Moreover, because I long ago stopped caring what politicians and the media say about me, I was also better able to make the hard decisions that might make my powerful neighbors mad.

Those who helped our Court to run smoothly and professionally, in the long run helped create a culture in the early Republic where, by and large, the Court's judgments were enforced by those other branches of government, even when those other branches were the losers. The Supreme Court is only as effective as people think it is. When in 1832 the Supreme Court decided *Worcester v. Georgia*[37] —a case in which the Court took sides with the Cherokees against the state of Georgia—Georgia simply ignored the Court's ruling. President Andrew Jackson is famously

said to have challenged the Court to come enforce its ruling itself! He probably never said that,[38] but the implication, the idea
is sound: The Court's only weapon is its moral authority. This
moral authority of the Supreme Court was a long time in the
making, and once it became established, it built on itself little by
little.

This is an accomplishment that entitles John Marshall to his
place together with such figures as Hammurabi, Grotius, and
Confucius in the frieze of great lawgivers that frames the courtroom where the Supreme Court Justices sit. Marshall and his
contemporaries helped fulfill President Washington's vision of
the Court and build the "pillar upon which our national Government [rests]."[39]

ITINERANT JUSTICE
Riding Circuit

I N JUNE 1798, DURING THE JOHN ADAMS ADMINISTRATION,
Supreme Court Justice James Iredell wrote a letter to Secretary of State Timothy Pickering: "I very unfortunately was
prevented [from] reaching Savannah," wrote Justice Iredell, "by
one of the greatest floods of rain ever known in this State, which
met me on my Journey." "[This flood]," Iredell continued, "rendered it impossible for me to proceed any considerable distance,
all the bridges almost being broke up in every direction. . . . I
made every effort in my power, and was nearly drowned in the
attempt, but was obliged at length absolutely to desist. . . ."[1] Iredell was explaining his failure to reach Savannah, Georgia,
where he was slated to preside over the federal court for the
Southern Circuit. To add insult to injury, the local papers soon
took Justice Iredell to task for his supposedly negligent failure to
attend.

Few people realize that, for much of the Supreme Court's
first century, one of the Justices' primary duties was to serve as
roving trial judges in the lower federal courts. From 1789 to 1891,
the Justices were required by law to "ride circuit." They traveled

thousands of miles each year to preside over trials and intermediate appeals all over the country. In fact, the Justices spent a lot more time riding circuit than they did hearing cases at the Supreme Court.

It's just remarkable, if you think about it. Just imagine the nine justices today running around the country, holding court from Boston to Baton Rouge. And then going back to Washington to hear appeals from their own decisions!

The history of circuit-riding is a window on both the living conditions and many of the great events of the founding era. And it turns out that we can learn a lot from the century-long debate over circuit-riding—about changes in the Supreme Court's role over time and about the enduring value of bringing the Court to the people.

ARTICLE III OF THE Constitution vests the "judicial Power of the United States" in "one supreme Court, and in such inferior Courts as the Congress may from time to time ordain and establish." Today, of course, we have a three-tier system of federal courts. There are the district courts, which are the federal trial courts. Then there are the U.S. Courts of Appeals, which are the intermediate appellate courts. And, finally, there's the Supreme Court—which has the proverbial last word.

But for the first eleven months of the United States' existence, the country had no federal judiciary at all. It wasn't until the Judiciary Act of 1789 that Congress first established the federal courts. The 1789 act set the number of Supreme Court Justices at six. It created one federal district court for each of the states in the Union — each to be presided over by a single district judge. And most important, the act established three "circuit" courts— covering the eastern, middle, and southern regions of the country, respectively.

But, lest there be any confusion, the circuit courts of that era were nothing like today's U.S. Courts of Appeals, which are also designated by circuit. The circuit courts created in 1789—and which continued to exist in one form or another for the next 120 years—were primarily trial courts. They had original jurisdiction over major federal criminal cases, meaning that such cases could start in the circuit courts rather than reaching them only on appeal. And, together with the district courts, they had concurrent jurisdiction over lesser criminal cases and most civil trials. The circuit courts' appellate role, by contrast, was rather limited.

Perhaps more surprising, the 1789 act did not provide for judges whose job was exclusively to sit on these new circuit courts. Instead, the six Justices of the Supreme Court and the district judges were given double duty as circuit court judges. In each of the three new circuits, two Justices would be assigned to "ride circuit" twice a year—holding court together with the district judge in each state. That was no small task, for the territory to be covered was vast, the travel grueling, and the accommodations far from commodious.

What accounts for Congress's decision to give the Justices of the Supreme Court a dual role as itinerant trial judges? Good old-fashioned Yankee frugality was certainly one big reason. The new republic was cash poor and heavily indebted, and Congress no doubt saw circuit-riding as a way to get two courts for the price of one. This penny-pinching wasn't altogether unreasonable. As it turned out, the Justices' duties at the Supreme Court itself fell far short of a full-time job at first. The Court's business was minimal initially. It decided no more than sixty cases in its first ten years. That's compared with nearly a hundred each year today!

But pecuniary concerns certainly weren't the only reason for circuit-riding. From the beginning, circuit-riding was viewed as a vital means of bringing the Supreme Court to the people. When Congress passed the 1789 act, the United States was less than a year old. In many states, the Constitution had been ratified by only the narrowest of margins. And the creation of a federal judiciary had been one of the most contentious aspects of the new system. In short, the new republic was still on pretty shaky ground. There was a lot of work to be done if her founding charter—and her federal courts—were to earn the trust and respect of her citizens.

Many in the founding generation thought circuit-riding would aid in this endeavor. By assigning the Justices of the Supreme Court a central role in the circuit courts, the supporters of circuit-riding hoped to enhance the legitimacy of the lower federal courts.

First of all, the Justices' participation was supposed to improve the quality and uniformity of lower-court decision-making. The Supreme Court would be present—in living color, so to speak—to keep the new federal courts all across the country in line. Circuit-riding was also meant to make the lower courts' decisions more final. After all, how important is it to take your appeal to the Supreme Court itself, when a Supreme Court Justice has already overseen your trial? As Senator William Paterson of New Jersey put it in 1789, circuit-riding allowed the Justices to "meet every citizen in his [the citizen's] own State—not *drag* him *800 miles* [on] an appeal."[2]

Perhaps most important, circuit-riding made the Justices ambassadors of the new national government. Nowadays, we see the President and other national officials on television daily, and the federal government maintains a presence throughout the country. But during the founding era, in most areas of the country the circuit-riding Justices were the only representatives of the central government with whom the public had regular contact. In other words, it was the Justices, through their connections with lawyers, litigants, and leaders across the country, who gave the federal government a human face. And it was a pretty good face, too! Men like Chief Justice John Marshall clearly had the power to inspire confidence in the new republic.

In the course of their circuit-riding duties, the Justices campaigned vigorously for the new Constitution and the new national government. They did so most famously through their grand jury charges. One of the Justices' duties upon convening the circuit court was to impanel a grand jury to hear criminal charges. The Justices would then deliver a "charge" to the jury—an often lengthy oration that was part legal tutorial, part moral sermon, and part political speech. Imagine the setting. In those days, grand juries were hand-selected, so the Justices were speaking directly to the leaders of the community. And holding court was a big public event, so the crowds were listening and the Justices' speeches were often published in local newspapers.

The Justices did instruct the jurors on the law, of course. But what's so remarkable about these jury charges, to our modern ears, is their overtly political character. I sometimes tell audiences that I like to give speeches about history because it's less dangerous than talking about the present. Well, the early Justices were much braver than I! Throughout the country's tempestuous first decades, they used their jury charges to address the great political and legal controversies of the day. Indeed, the Justices sometimes went too far. It was an incendiary grand jury charge that led to the only impeachment of a Supreme Court Justice—Samuel Chase—in our country's history; Chase had charged a Baltimore grand jury that Congress's repeal of the Judiciary Act of 1801 would "take away all security for property and personal liberty, and our Republican constitution will sink into a mobocracy."[3] But the Justices also consistently—and often eloquently—advocated the importance of a strong central government in securing the rights and liberties of the people. Citizens from all across the country listened to those speeches, and I suspect the effect on public opinion was significant.

* * *

WHATEVER THE PERCEIVED VIRTUES of circuit-riding, it presented severe problems from the beginning. It imposed a crushing burden on the Justices of the Supreme Court. Whereas the Justices spent only six weeks of each year hearing cases at the Supreme Court itself, it took many of them six months to ride the circuits. During this time, most were separated from their families. They traveled by horse and carriage over rough roads and through foul weather, for thousands of miles each year. Most stayed in taverns while on the road, and they were sometimes forced to share rooms with unsavory characters. Astonishingly, the Justices paid the entire expense of their travels out of their own meager salaries.

The hardships were greatest for those assigned to the vast and rustic Southern Circuit, which covered Georgia and the Carolinas. Justice James Iredell of North Carolina was relegated to this duty for many years. His letters to his wife, Hannah, tell of the perils and pains of the road. In one letter from Granville County, North Carolina, in 1791, Justice Iredell lamented that the "accommodations were in some places very bad," complaining of "a very rascally house" where he was "obliged to put up . . . a parcel of worthless young Fellows . . . sitting up drinking gaming & cursing and swearing all night."[4] Two months later, he wrote from New Bern, North Carolina, to tell Hannah that he had been robbed by a "Scoundrel" on the road who had "unstrapped my Portmanteau from behind the Chair."[5] The following April, he wrote from Savannah, Georgia, that he had been thrown off by his horse and run over by a wheel of the carriage, leaving his leg "in so much pain" that he was obliged to stay "very inconveniently at a house on the road."[6] In April 1798, from Williamston, North Carolina, he described his treacherous crossing of a "very long Swamp that had a most formidable appearance," punctuated by very deep holes where a bridge had collapsed.[7] And I thought the Washington, D.C., traffic was dangerous! I must say, it is truly humbling to consider the extraordinary sacrifices these early Justices and their families made for our country.

The hardships of circuit-riding were so great, in fact, that they drove many a Justice to early resignation or even early death. Justice Iredell died at the age of forty-eight, worn-out after eight years of riding the Southern Circuit. Justice Thomas Johnson resigned in 1793 after a mere six months on the bench. "I cannot resolve," Justice Johnson wrote to President Washington, "to spend six Months in the Year of the few I may have left [away] from my Family, on Roads at Taverns chiefly and often in Situations where the most moderate Desires are disappointed."[8]

Nor were these hardships the only problems with circuit-riding. Indeed, many of the early Justices believed that the circuit system was unconstitutional. For one thing, it presented the unseemly prospect that a Supreme Court Justice might hear an appeal from a judgment that he himself had rendered as a circuit justice. Even if a Justice were to recuse himself from a case he had decided below, the remaining Justices might be disinclined to offend their absent colleague by reversing his ruling. In addition, many thought that, by assigning the Justices to the separate posts of circuit judges, Congress had usurped the President's exclusive power to appoint federal judges.

AND SO IT SHOULD COME as no surprise that the Justices unanimously and vigorously opposed circuit-riding from the start. The early Justices were seasoned politicians, and, with the help of George Washington and others, they campaigned vigorously throughout the 1790s to have Congress abolish circuit-riding. But it was not until the Judiciary Act of 1801, when John Adams was President, that Congress finally acted. The 1801 act eliminated the Justices' circuit-riding duties and established six new circuit courts to be overseen by sixteen new judges.

This was not a politically neutral reform, and the uproar it generated brought circuit-riding back in less than a year. If you think the contemporary battles over judicial appointments are contentious, consider this story.

Soon after the 1801 act was passed, in the final days of President John Adams's administration, Thomas Jefferson's Republicans denounced it as a Federalist scheme to pack the new circuit courts with Federalist appointees. And, indeed, within just two short weeks, the Federalist-dominated Senate confirmed President Adams's nominations for all sixteen of the new circuit judges. These were some of the so-called "midnight judges" of *Marbury v. Madison* fame. But with the inauguration of Thomas Jefferson and the new Republican Congress, the Republicans took control, and soon repealed the 1801 act. The Repeal Act eliminated the sixteen new circuit judgeships. And, as if to chastise the Federalists then sitting on the Supreme Court, it restored the Justices' loathsome circuit-riding duties!

In one stroke, the Republicans had dismissed sixteen sitting federal judges, all of them appointed by the opposing party. Can you imagine the scandal? I don't think anything in modern history even comes close. But the Republicans' next move was even more brazen. To prevent the Supreme Court from striking down the Repeal Act as unconstitutional, Congress simply canceled the Court's next Term!

By the time the Court did confront a constitutional challenge to the Repeal Act, brought by a plaintiff more than a year later, the uproar had settled. By then Chief Justice John Marshall and the other Justices had privately agreed that the Repeal Act was unconstitutional, but they wanted to avoid a showdown with the Republican Congress and with President Jefferson. So, in an apparent triumph of pragmatism over principle, the Court upheld the Repeal Act in its 1803 decision in *Stuart v. Laird*.[9] Remarkably, the Court simply ignored the plaintiff's objection to Congress's dismissal of the sixteen Federalist circuit judges. I don't think the Court would get away with that today! As for the plaintiff's challenge to the circuit-riding system, the Court said that it had gone along with circuit-riding for so long that it could not now strike it down.

It was less than a year after the Repeal Act that, Justice Samuel Chase got himself into hot water with his fiery grand jury charge. In the course of instructing the jurors, Chase ranted against the Repeal Act and decried recent developments in his home state of Maryland. " [T]he abolition of the office of the sixteen circuit judges," Chase declared, "has already . . . shaken" "the independence of the national judiciary . . . to its foundation."[10] Moreover, Chase told the jurors, the recent amendment of the Maryland state constitution to allow universal suffrage, "will, in my opinion, certainly and rapidly destroy all protection to property, and all security to personal liberty, and our Republican constitution will sink into a *mobocracy,* the *worst* of all possible governments."[11]

It didn't take long for President Jefferson to get wind of this speech. Jefferson soon wrote to his allies in the House of Representatives, suggesting that Chase be impeached. In due course, the House passed eight separate articles of impeachment against Chase. Most of them involved his alleged partiality in two high-profile trials over which he had presided while riding circuit. Ultimately, the Senate acquitted Chase of all these charges. But the charge on which the Senate came closest to convicting was that Chase, in his 1803 charge to the Baltimore grand jury, had "prostituted the high judicial character with which he was invested, to the low purpose of an electioneering partizan." Just four more votes would have secured Chase's removal from office.[12] Floods and fatigue, it seems, were not the only perils faced by the circuit-riding Justices.

* * *

FOR THE NEXT SEVENTY years, circuit-riding remained a part of the Supreme Court Justices' duties. These duties were less onerous for some than for others. And they often afforded the Justices great autonomy in charting the course of the law. Justice Joseph Story, who was the circuit justice for the First Circuit for most of the first half of the nineteenth century, appears to have relished this office. "[I]f my name shall happen to go down to posterity," Story wrote to a friend in 1840, "my character as a Judge will be more fully [and] accurately seen in the opinions of the Circuit Court than in the Supreme Court. In the former I speak for myself after full research [and] elaborate consideration [and] in the exercise of my own free judgment. In the latter I speak for the Court, [and] my free Judgments are modified, controlled [and] sometimes fettered by the necessary obedience to the opinions of my Brethren."[13]

What Justice Story said was especially true because, in those days, the Justices almost never issued more than one, unanimous opinion.

Despite the opportunities that circuit-riding presented, its attendant problems only increased with the passage of time. Transportation improved, of course. But as the country expanded, so did the number of circuits and the territory the Justices had to cover. With the addition of each new circuit, a new Justice was added to the Supreme Court to ride it. By 1838, the number of circuits had increased to nine. That year, Justice McKinley's duties on the Ninth Circuit—which then comprised Alabama, Louisiana, Mississippi, and Arkansas—required him to travel an astounding ten thousand miles.[14] This before airplanes! But even more problematic was the incredible growth in the caseload of the Supreme Court and the circuit courts. The time consumed by riding circuit made it ever more difficult for the Justices to manage their docket at the Supreme Court.

In the face of these difficulties, attempts to abolish circuit-riding continued throughout the nineteenth century. But Congress steadfastly rebuffed these efforts. One is tempted to chalk this up to foolish obstinacy, and that may be as good an explanation as any. But the congressional debates over circuit-riding also reveal genuine concerns about the role of the Supreme Court and Supreme Court Justices in our nation. In essence, these legislators feared that the Justices would be corrupted by Washington, D.C.; that they would lose touch with the reality of trial courts; and that they would lose all connection with the states and with ordinary people from around the country. Here's some of what they had to say.

Back in the nineteenth century, just like today, legislators liked to fulminate against the ill effects of Washington, D.C., on the public officials who reside there. Speaking on the floor of Congress in 1819, Senator William Smith of South Carolina predicted that, if the Justices were relieved of their circuit-riding duties, they would become "completely cloistered within the city of Washington, and their decisions, instead of emanating from enlarged and liberal minds, will assume a severe and local character."[15]

Others predicted that the Justices, if permitted to remain in the capital, would fall under the pernicious influence of Washington lawyers.

My personal favorite is Senator Abner Lacock of Pennsylvania, who explained how the Justices' *old age* would contribute to this problem. "*Old men,*" Lacock warned, "are often impatient of contradiction, frequently *vain* and *susceptible to flattery*. The weaknesses incident to old age will be *discovered* and *practiced upon* by the lawyer willing to make the most of his profession, and located in the same city, holding daily and familiar intercourse with the judge. . . . The judges, bowed down by the weight of years, will be willing to find a staff to lean upon; and thus the opinion of the *Washington Bar* is made the *law of the land*."[16] Senator Lacock was just a spring chicken—forty-nine years old—when he wrote those words! I can tell you from personal experience that he knew virtually nothing of the effects of age. And, I might add, he greatly overestimated the guile of Washington lawyers.

But it was not just fear of Washington's influence that kept circuit-riding alive so long. Throughout the years, legislators predicted that ending circuit-riding would estrange the Justices from the states. "Alienate the judges from the States," declared Representative James Bowlin of Missouri in 1848, "consolidate the Court in the metropolis, and the day is not far distant, when the sovereign rights of the free States of this Confederacy will be swallowed up in this mighty vortex of power."[17]

Others expressed the belief that circuit-riding made the Justices better judges by exposing them to the people and to the workings of trial courts. If circuit-riding were abolished, warned Senator George Badger of North Carolina, "We shall have these gentlemen as judges of the Supreme Court not seen by the people of the United States—not known and recognized by them . . . ; but sitting here alone—becoming philosophical and speculative in their inquiries as to law—becoming necessarily more and more dim as to the nature of the law of the various States . . . unseen, final arbiters of justice, issuing their decrees as it were from a secret chamber. . . ."[18]

Despite these impassioned defenses of circuit-riding, the growing workload of the Supreme Court ultimately brought the practice to an end. By the 1880s, the Court had more than a thousand cases on its docket. Despite the Justices' Herculean efforts, they could not keep up—the Court was an astounding three years behind in its work. In 1891, Congress at last addressed this crisis in the Evarts Act. The act created the U.S. Courts of Appeals to oversee the circuits, thus inaugurating the three-tier system of federal courts we have today.

It also established discretionary Supreme Court review by "writ of certiorari," which is an order by which the Supreme

Court opts to review a lower-court decision on appeal. When a court decides to hear an appeal, it is said to "grant certiorari."

But far more important for present purposes, Congress at long last relieved the Justices of their circuit-riding duties. After more than a century on the road, the members of the Supreme Court could finally dedicate themselves exclusively to their work at the Court itself.

THE END OF CIRCUIT-riding did not, of course, bring an end to debates over the proper role of the Supreme Court and of Supreme Court Justices. Indeed, many of the concerns expressed by the historical defenders of circuit-riding are echoed in contemporary commentary on the Supreme Court. "Our Supreme Court Justices are isolated in a marble palace in Washington," wrote then-dean Erwin Griswold of Harvard Law School in 1960.[19] Griswold lamented the lack of opportunities for open dialogue between the Justices and members of the bar around the country—and he surmised that this detracted from the possibility of genuinely constructive commentary on the Court's work.

More recently, scholars have opined that the Justices are out of touch with public values and the realities of the lower courts—and that this makes them ill-suited to decide the great constitutional issues of our day.[20] Professor Akhil Amar of Yale has even argued that some version of circuit-riding should be reinstituted. "[I]t would not be a bad thing," Amar says, "to get the justices outside the Beltway from time to time to sit with fellow federal judges elsewhere in the country in order to make them more attentive to state law and different perspectives in this vast country of ours." And the Justices should preside over criminal trials from time to time, Amar says, because it would give us a chance to see up close the real-world effects of the Court's criminal procedure decisions.[21]

Yet another professor, John McGinnis of Northwestern, has

suggested that, instead of reviving circuit-riding, we should instead have "Supreme Court riding." Instead of having the Supreme Court Justices do rotating duty on the lower courts, McGinnis suggests that we get rid of the Justices altogether and have lower-court judges sit in rotation on the Supreme Court. The lower-court judges could be randomly assigned to hear cases on the Supreme Court for half a year or a year at a time. Just as the circuit-riding Justices of history brought the Court to the people, the lower-court judges of today would bring the people to the Court.[22]

None of this is likely to happen, of course. But these discussions do reveal that the concerns expressed by the defenders of circuit-riding—about the need for connection between the Supreme Court and the rest of the country—are current concerns as well.

WE DO STILL RETAIN some remnants of the old circuit system. Most notably, each of the Justices is assigned responsibility for one or more of the thirteen federal circuits. For example, I was assigned to the Ninth Circuit. My responsibilities included keeping abreast of executions scheduled in states in the Ninth Circuit and summarizing any requests to stay the executions filed with the Supreme Court for the other Justices. The circuit justices have authority to decide emergency-stay applications and other motions for temporary relief originating within their respective circuits. For instance, a party to a case might ask the Supreme Court to "stay" a lower court's ruling—that is, prevent it from going into effect—until it has had the chance to file a petition for certiorari. And circuit justices maintain active relationships with the judges in their circuits, frequently attending judicial conferences of lawyers and judges in their areas and so forth.

But the era of riding circuit is now long past, and that is a good thing. Constitutional problems aside, the idea of traveling hither and yon as an itinerant trial judge, even with the conveniences of modern transportation and communication, is unworkable and unattractive. The Supreme Court is now a very busy place—and being a Supreme Court Justice is at least a full-time job!

Nevertheless, we should be grateful for the efforts and sacrifices of the circuit-riding Justices, especially those of the founding era. By defending the Constitution and by helping to secure the role of the Supreme Court, they paved the way for all that the Justices do now. Nevertheless, the values long associated with circuit-riding are crucial—and we must continue to advance them in other ways. The role of the Justices makes it indispensable that they stay in touch with the concerns faced by the lower courts, the legal profession, the states, and, perhaps most important, the people.

THE SUPREME COURT'S
CHANGING JURISDICTION

———————//———————

O
N MY FIRST DAY SERVING AS A SUPREME COURT JUSTICE, I
walked into my new chambers at the Court and was
greeted by staggering mounds of papers strewn across
the floor. It was quite a welcome! Hundreds of appeals to the
Supreme Court had accumulated over the summer recess—
appeals that I had a mere number of days to review with my law
clerks before the Justices convened for the first Conference of the
Term.[1] At the Conference, I was to meet with the other eight Justices and discuss which among those stacks of appeals, known as
petitions for certiorari, warranted the Court's review.

That was my first taste of the Supreme Court's certiorari process. When I first joined the Court, the Court was taking some
159 cases a year.[2] These days the Court hears around ninety
cases a year. The Justices select those ninety cases out of approximately eight *thousand* petitions for certiorari. We have long
grown accustomed to the notion that the Supreme Court has the
power to pick and choose which cases to decide and thereby set
its own agenda. But that was not always the case.

*   *   *

FOR THE FIRST CENTURY of its existence, the Supreme Court had no discretion over its caseload. Those were the days of "mandatory jurisdiction": virtually every appeal to the Court had to be resolved. Article III of the Constitution confers Congress with the power to make "Exceptions" and "Regulations" to the Supreme Court's "appellate Jurisdiction,"[3] and in those early days, Congress played a dominant role in setting forth the bounds of which cases and controversies the Supreme Court would decide. Congress, for instance, insulated federal criminal convictions from Supreme Court review until 1889.[4] Meanwhile, Congress provided that the Supreme Court was obligated to hear certain judgments of lower federal courts and of the highest state courts implicating or involving the Constitution, treaties, or federal laws.[5] As soon as any such case reached the Court by way of a "writ of error," the Justices were obligated to resolve the merits of each case.[6] That was true irrespective of how negligible the national significance of the issue or how meritless the claim.

With such a large mandatory docket, the Court soon found itself inundated. In 1860, the Supreme Court had 310 cases on its docket and issued decisions in 91. In 1870, the Court had 636 cases on its docket and issued decisions in 280. In 1880, the Court found itself with 1,202 cases on its docket and issued decisions in 365.[7] The early Justices found themselves falling years behind and struggling to efficiently process their caseload. Some litigants found themselves waiting for three years before they could be heard.[8]

In 1891, Congress stepped in to resolve the crisis.[9] First, as mentioned, Congress created what we now know as the U.S. Courts of Appeals. It was Congress's hope that a system of intermediate federal appellate courts would deter parties from seeking Supreme Court review, though those expectations were later dashed. Congress also introduced the now-familiar writ of certiorari. Certiorari enabled the Court to sift through federal appellate court decisions in diversity, patent, revenue, criminal, and admiralty cases, determine which ones were of sufficient importance to warrant review, and exert greater control over its docket.[10] Nonetheless, the mandatory appeal docket—those cases that the Court was required to take—was still four times the size of the discretionary certiorari docket. Appeals continued to pile up.[11]

THE BALANCE DRAMATICALLY SHIFTED with the passage of the Judiciary Act of 1925, commonly referred to as the Judges' Bill. Chief Justice William Howard Taft was the mastermind behind the legislation from start to finish. A decade earlier, in the wake of losing his 1912 presidential reelection bid, Taft had already called for the Court's mandatory jurisdiction to be limited to "questions of constitutional construction."[12] He was deeply committed to broadening the Court's discretion over the cases it would hear. In Taft's view, at least 60 percent of the Court's cases lacked any merit and the Court itself should decide which cases were important enough to require a decision.[13]

At the start of the October 1921 Term, Taft appointed Justices Day, Van Devanter, and McReynolds to a committee responsible for crafting a bill that would reform the Court's jurisdiction.[14] Taft reportedly went so far as to recommend which senators should be placed on the Senate Judiciary Committee to best ensure the bill's smooth passage.[15] He rallied his fellow Justices to support the bill and arranged for their testimony before Congress, aggressively solicited the support of the American Bar Association, and even negotiated compromises in the legislation with Montana senator Thomas Walsh and New York senator Royal Copeland.[16]

Taft's extraordinary push was successful. The Judges' Bill passed and, in hindsight, we can see that 1925 marked the birth of the modern Supreme Court.[17]

The bill rendered the majority of the Court's docket discretionary. It removed the possibility of direct appeal to the Supreme Court in most circumstances and transferred substantial numbers of appeals to the certiorari process.[18] And in 1988, Congress eliminated nearly all the residual elements of mandatory jurisdiction.[19] Today, with only the most minor of exceptions, the Supreme Court is effectively an "all-certiorari tribunal" with full control of its docket.[20]

Remarkably, the criteria that govern grants of certiorari have remained relatively constant over time. At the turn of the twentieth century, the Court emphasized "the necessity of restraint in granting writs of certiorari," declaring "that it was only in cases of 'gravity and general importance' or 'to secure uniformity of decision' that the certiorari power should be exercised."[21] Those same fundamental principles of restraint bind the Court today. The Supreme Court Rules caution that "[r]eview on a writ of certiorari is not a matter of right"[22] and that petitions are "rarely granted when the asserted error consists of erroneous factual findings or the misapplication of a properly stated rule of law."[23] Rather, the Court requires more pressing reasons, such as a conflict of authority among the lower courts and a significant question of federal law, before it will order full briefing and oral argument on the merits.

AS NOTED EARLIER, THE Court today receives approximately 8,000 petitions, a striking increase from the 5,144 petitions the Court received in 1980 and the 1,321 it received in 1950.[24] It grants a mere 1.125 percent—around ninety—each year. The petitions come from a wide range of litigants, from corporations represented by major law firms to prisoners filing handwritten appeals on their own. They appeal from decisions from both state and federal courts across the country. And they run the gamut of legal issues, ranging from questions about complex regulatory schemes set up by federal administrative agencies, to a rancher's land dispute.

The Court has many internal streamlining processes in place to process the petitions. Most of the Justices have joined a "cert pool," whereby each of their law clerks is assigned a number of petitions for which to prepare screening memoranda that are circulated among all the Justices, thus pooling their resources and avoiding duplicative efforts.[25] When a single Justice, upon reviewing the initial memorandum, believes a case may warrant review, it is listed for discussion at the Conference; all others are filtered out expeditiously. Daunted as I may have been that first day that I entered my chambers and saw the stacks of petitions, I soon found that the Court manages to process petitions in a timely and efficient manner. Long gone are the days when litigants would wait for years in vain for any word from the Court.

No process is perfect. I like to think, however, that today's Supreme Court Justices, freed of the strictures of mandatory appeals, are able to focus and carefully consider the most important, difficult, and pressing legal issues of the time.

GOLDEN TONGUES

Oral Advocacy Before the Court

———//———

Lawyers who appear before the Supreme Court are often somewhat intimidated by the powers the Justices wield. Because it is the Court's written opinions that establish the law, it often seems that the Court deliberates about the legal principles, writes the opinions, and delivers its judgments without any outside assistance. It may seem that lawyers exist only to digest and apply the law laid down by the Court.

But the communication between Justices and advocates flows two ways. While the Justices answer the legal questions raised by the parties, the vibrancy of our case law depends upon the assistance the Court receives from the lawyers who appear before it. Lawyers identify and spell out the legal issues. They offer ways to resolve those issues. And at oral argument, they assist the Justices in the task of synthesizing opposing viewpoints.

As the late Chief Justice William H. Rehnquist said, "My colleagues and I disagree among ourselves about many legal questions, but I think that we would all agree that a poorly presented case is apt to be a poorly decided case; therefore, we have reason to hope that litigants before us will do a good job."[1]

Oral advocates are charged with the unenviable duty of looking up at nine Justices, each with his or her own significant questions and views about the best way to answer those questions. Oral advocates must present the Court with the strongest arguments in favor of their clients' positions, while simultaneously recognizing their responsibility to the Court and the country to help shape a consistent, coherent body of law. They must often juggle two or three different lines of questioning in their heads in order to successfully respond to each Justice's individual concerns.

WHEN THE SUPREME COURT first sat, it undoubtedly faced a multitude of tasks. But given the importance of legal counsel both to the parties who relied upon them and to the Justices who trusted them to present the cases, it is hardly surprising that the first act taken by the Court was admitting lawyers to its practice. On February 5, 1790, only two days after the Justices first met in open session, the first three advocates were admitted to practice before the court. During that term, twenty-five additional men were admitted to practice before the Supreme Court. In the next term, another twenty-nine were admitted. If those numbers seem small, the decade that followed was even more surprising: On average, only five attorneys were admitted per year.

In the Court's early days in Philadelphia and Washington, the Supreme Court bar was "a club-like group of local counsel who handled cases in the Court upon referral from counsel elsewhere."[2] It was not unusual for members of Congress to appear before the Court to argue on behalf of private litigants.[3]

Matters have changed significantly since those early days. The Court has averaged around 4,300 new attorney admissions per year over the last twenty years, more than a hundredfold increase from 1790.

In part, more lawyers have been admitted to practice because our country has grown substantially larger and legal issues have increased in number and in complexity. Just as the first Court could not function until it admitted members of the bar, a history of the Court would be incomplete if it did not look at the relationship that oral advocacy has had with the Court. Oral advocates have helped strengthen the Supreme Court. Without their contributions, our jurisprudence would be poorer.

The most controversial case that the Court decided in its infancy was *Chisholm v. Georgia,* in 1793.[4] Executor Alexander Chisholm claimed the state of Georgia had failed to pay the estate of South Carolina merchant Captain Robert Farquhar for goods he'd delivered during the Revolutionary War. U.S. Attorney General Edmund Randolph argued Chisholm's case before the Supreme Court. The issue presented—whether Georgia was immune to suit as a sovereign entity—was fundamental in determining the power of state governments in our newly developing nation.

In 1793, only two attorneys were admitted to practice before the Supreme Court. *Chisholm* was argued before the appointment of Chief Justice John Marshall; it was decided before the seminal cases that helped shape the Supreme Court's role in our country, such as *Marbury v. Madison.* The country had not yet recognized the importance of the Court. And so perhaps we can excuse Georgia for not sending a top-notch attorney. It is, however, a little surprising that Georgia elected to send nobody. Georgia was unrepresented by counsel at argument.

It is evident from the opinion that the Court agonized over the question as faithfully as if Georgia had been present. But the matter was difficult. Because it failed to present the opposing view, the odds were slanted against Georgia from the start. It lost. The Court ruled that federal courts could hear cases in law or equity brought by private citizens against states and that states did not enjoy so-called sovereign immunity—protection from being sued—from suits brought by citizens of other states.

In the hue and cry that followed, Congress intervened and passed the Eleventh Amendment to overrule the decision. The amendment stands for the principle of sovereign immunity, providing that the "Judicial power . . . shall not be construed to extend to any suit in law or equity, commenced or prosecuted against one of the United States by Citizens of another State, or by Citizens or Subjects of any Foreign State." And since that day, parties with cases pending before the Court have sent the best legal advocate they can find.

One prominent lawyer who often appeared before the Court in the early days of our nation was William Pinkney. Like many excellent oral advocates who followed in his footsteps, Pinkney served as the Attorney General of the United States.[5] His specialty was maritime law. Because he started his legal career shortly before war broke out with Britain in 1812, you can imagine that he did a brisk business. He argued eighty-four cases before the Supreme Court.

One of Pinkney's most important cases was *Schooner Exchange v. McFaddon*.[6] In that case, a ship owned by Maryland merchants was commandeered into the French navy. When the ship landed in Philadelphia, its American owners clamored for its return. Needless to say, the case had important international implications for our fledgling country. On the one hand, a foreign government had taken the property of American citizens. On the other hand, international relationships with France could suffer if the courts ruled against it. Pinkney, at the request of the President, presented the case for the French government.

The case was difficult. In delivering the opinion, Chief Justice Marshall recognized that he was "exploring an unbeaten path, with few, if any, aids from precedents or written law."[7] Marshall's only guide in crafting that landmark opinion was the oral argument that Pinkney delivered. In presenting the case to the court, Pinkney argued that "when wrongs are inflicted by one nation upon another, in tempestuous times, they cannot be redressed by the judicial department. The right to demand redress belongs to the executive department, which alone represents the sovereignty of the nation."[8]

Chief Justice Marshall's opinion for the Court in *Schooner Exchange* still serves as a bedrock case in international law.[9] That opinion specifically held that U.S. courts lacked jurisdiction over the ship of a foreign state found in a U.S. port, though the case is commonly cited by the Court and other nations for the broader principle that foreign sovereigns enjoy immunity from suit in U.S. courts. Marshall's opinion gives credit to Attorney General Pinkney's fine oral argument; Marshall ended his opinion by stating, "If this opinion be correct, there seems to be a necessity for admitting that the fact may be disclosed to the Court by the suggestion of the Attorney for the United States."[10] Such accolades are rarely given by the Supreme Court, and Pinkney must have worn that one proudly. While the Court rarely recognizes advocates in the text of its opinions, Pinkney was only one in a long line of lawyers who have helped guide the Court through murky doctrine and confusing legal issues.

Pinkney typically conducted his oral arguments in court in a fine style. He dressed flamboyantly, and his manner was so proud that he was accused of arrogance and conceit. On one particular occasion, an opponent believed Pinkney had treated him with contempt.[11] This young man confronted Pinkney and explained that he had been insulted by Pinkney's manner. Shocked and surprised, Pinkney agreed to apologize the next morning in Court.

The young man who demanded Pinkney's respect was none other than Daniel Webster—quite possibly the only oral advocate whose reputation tops that of Pinkney. Webster enjoyed an extremely successful and varied career in politics, including stints as a United States senator and secretary of state. But Webster's most lasting achievement was arguably his oral arguments before the Supreme Court. Webster argued nearly two hundred cases before the Court. His skills, accomplishments, and influence as an advocate were widely admired. Seth Waxman, who served as Solicitor General under President Clinton, has put the point vividly: "In the realm of advocacy, Webster doesn't merely sit in the Pantheon: He is Zeus himself."[12] Though Webster was known to

Photographic print of Daniel Webster.

pepper his arguments "with classical allusions and rhetorical flourishes," he was also known for his ability to marshal precedents and historical evidence with skill.[13]

Among the prominent cases argued in the early nineteenth century, Webster argued *McCulloch v. Maryland,* which clarified the federal government's implied powers to pass laws to implement the Constitution's express powers in order to create a functional national government.[14] Webster also argued *Gibbons v. Ogden,* a critical case about the scope of Congress's power under the Commerce Clause.[15] All of these important cases are still taught in law schools across the nation because they shed light on the constitutional bounds of the federal government's powers.

In no oral argument, however, were Webster's considerable oral gifts on better display than when he argued *Dartmouth College v. Woodward* in 1818.[16] As a graduate of Dartmouth College, Webster had a keen interest in defending his beloved alma mater. After the president of Dartmouth College was deposed by the college's trustees, the New Hampshire legislature sought to force the college to become a public institution. To determine whether the New Hampshire legislature's action was valid, the Court had to determine whether Dartmouth's private corporate charter qualified as a "contract" under the Constitution's Contracts Clause, which prohibits states from enacting laws that impair contract rights.

Webster opened his argument in *Dartmouth College* with the following sentence: "Eleemosynary corporations are for the management of private property, according to the will of the donors."[17]

This simple opening was followed by a memorable conclusion: "Sir, you may destroy this institution; it is weak; it is in your hands! I know it is one of the lesser lights in the literary horizon of our country. You may put it out. But if you do so, you must carry through your work! You must extinguish, one after another, all those great lights of science which, for more than a century have thrown their radiance over our land! . . . It is, sir, as I have said, a small college—and yet there are those who love it."[18]

One contemporaneous observer commented: "[T]he feelings which [Webster] had thus far succeeded in keeping down broke forth. His lips quivered; his cheeks trembled with emotion; his eyes were filled with tears, his voice choked, and he seemed struggling to the utmost to gain that mastery over himself which might save him from an unmanly burst of feeling."[19] Webster closed his argument by analogizing the plight of Dartmouth College to the one confronted by Shakespeare's Julius Caesar: "When I see my Alma Mater surrounded, like Caesar in the senate-house, by those who are reiterating stab upon stab, I would not, for this right hand, have her turn to me, and say, Et tu quoque, mi filii! And thou too, my son!"

Webster was far from the only person in the courtroom who sought to suppress "unmanly" feelings. Chief Justice Marshall, not a person easily reduced to sentiment, was reported to have had his eyes fill with tears during Webster's presentation.[20] And Justice Joseph Story found Webster's presentation to be similarly moving. Indeed, Justice Story was so impressed with Webster's *Dartmouth College* argument that he suggested it was impossible to capture fully Webster's "manner and expression, glowing zeal, the brilliant terms of diction, the spontaneous bursts of rebuke . . . , the sparkling eye, the quivering lip, the speaking gesture, the ever changing, and ever moving tones of the voice, which add such strength and pathos and captivating enchantment to the orator as his words flow rapidly on during actual delivery."[21] Justice Story further recalled: "When Mr. Webster ceased to speak, it was some minutes before anyone seemed inclined to break the silence. The whole seemed but an agonizing dream, from which the audience was slowly and almost unconsciously awakening."[22] While I like to think that I have heard some excellent oral arguments at the Supreme Court, this description makes me wish I had the opportunity to hear Daniel Webster.

As one can tell from the description of Webster's oration in *Dartmouth College,* oral argument in the early days of the Supreme Court resembled nothing so much as entertainment. Charismatic oral advocates like Pinkney and Webster attracted large crowds and turned the Supreme Court into a social scene. A prominent legal historian has noted, "In the days before radio and television, the public appreciated a good trial and a good courtroom speech."[23] In the words of another historian, "the social season of Washington began with the opening of the Supreme Court term."[24]

One Supreme Court Justice wrote in 1812 that "[s]carcely a day passes in Court in which parties of ladies do not occasionally come in and hear, for a while, the arguments of learned counsel."[25] Webster reportedly stopped mid-sentence during an oral argument to accommodate a group of ladies who were just entering the courtroom.[26] Pinkney, meanwhile, is alleged to have ended one presentation by taking his seat and remarking with a grin: "that will do for the ladies."[27]

ORAL ADVOCATES TODAY ARE far more restrained than they were in Webster and Pinkney's time. No doubt the audiences are somewhat more staid as well. Indeed, if Webster were somehow able to view an oral argument at today's Court, there is a good chance he would barely recognize the event. During his era, oral argument often took hours, if not days. Indeed, the argument in *Dartmouth College* lasted three days, the argument in *Gibbons v. Ogden* lasted five days, and the argument in *McCulloch v. Maryland* lasted an incredible nine days. The Justices did not intervene with questions for counsel, and in those days there were few precedents to discuss. Freed of such constraints, advocates had more room to inject originality, emotion, and stylistic oratory.

Quantity, however, was not quality. Chief Justice Marshall purportedly once said that the "acme of judicial distinction means the ability to look a lawyer straight in the eyes for two hours and not hear a damned word he says."[28] This statement is apocryphal at best, but if it were true, it would explain why the Supreme Court eventually eliminated the practice of unlimited time for oral argument. The Court limited argument time to two hours per side in 1848, one hour per side in 1925, and finally thirty minutes per side in 1970—a practice that continues to this day.[29]

The prospect of time limits generated substantial debate. Some Justices opposed curtailing argument time. Chief Justice Roger Taney, for instance, worried that time limits would undercut the great tradition of oratory at the heart of American government and customary in contemporary political debates.[30] When the Court first passed an official Supreme Court rule limiting argument time to two hours, two Justices—James Moore Wayne and Levi Woodbury—publicly dissented. The Court's rising caseload, however, led to mounting pressures to curtail oral arguments that ultimately prevailed. With that change, the flamboyance of Pinkney and the days-long oratory of Webster ended. But the importance of oral arguments did not diminish.

Augustus Hill Garland, who served as Attorney General during the Cleveland administration, remembered the day that he was admitted as a young attorney to practice before the Supreme Court: "[A]s I stood up before the court and took the attorney's oath, my vision became disturbed and the judges all appeared to be, at least, twice the size they were, and more than double in number, and the surroundings generally appeared magnified in like proportion."[31] On that day, Garland listened to oral argument in two cases and remarked that the experience was "a feast not often spread before a young man struggling at the dim threshold of his profession."[32]

Garland went on to practice before the Supreme Court himself, once he got some experience under his belt. But his practice was interrupted by the most contentious time in our country's history—the Civil War. When he returned to Washington at the end of the conflict, the cases he had brought to the Court's attention shortly before hostilities began were still pending. He wanted to continue representing his clients, but there was a problem: In 1865, attorneys practicing in the United States courts were required to take an oath that they had not voluntarily supported any authority hostile to the United States. Under the Test Oath Act, any lawyer who had not been loyal to the North could not practice in the United States courts.[33]

Garland fought for his right to practice law before the Court. In December 1866, the Court declared the Test Oath Act unconstitutional and Garland was able to represent his clients in the cases that were pending. Garland won those cases for his clients, but the real victory for Garland—and for the Supreme Court—was more important than a handful of cases.

In one sense, Augustus Garland was very different from other talented oral advocates. He was not only a lawyer who argued in front of the Court; he had experienced the power of the Supreme Court firsthand as the beneficiary of its judgment. Garland's contribution to the Court, moreover, went beyond substantive legal matters. Besides his advocacy, he also published several books on Supreme Court practice.

Garland's familiarity with the Court led him to make several recommendations for the improvement of the practice of law. At the time, the Court had no page limits on briefs, and so attorneys took the chance to cram every last possible argument they could into the paperwork they filed with the Court. As Garland explained, "Not infrequently we see, not *briefs*, but long essays, even books in cases, drawing immensely upon the time of the court to wade through them."[34] However fulfilling those immense masterpieces may have been to the advocates who wrote them, they did little to help the Court focus its attention on the important issues in the case. More troubling, these voluminous briefs were filed a mere six days before argument. This left opponents three days to fashion a reply; as you can imagine, the usefulness of those briefs to the Court was limited at best.[35]

TODAY THE COURT HAS imposed word limits on briefs. Petitions for certiorari may not exceed 9,000 words, while the parties' briefs in cases scheduled for oral argument may not exceed 15,000 words.[36] Thus, not only does the clock run while advocates speak, but they must marshal their best arguments in their briefs well in advance of argument. (A party's opening brief is often submitted three months in advance of the argument.) This practice has served to hone and focus oral argument on the most important issues. It allows Justices to mull over the questions presented and prepare lines of inquiry that clarify and condense the issues in the case.

The increasing relevance of briefs has not rendered oral argument superfluous. By focusing attention on a few important issues, a good brief may sometimes lead to a great oral argument. For instance, Justice Robert H. Jackson was a gifted oral advocate when he served as Solicitor General from 1938 to 1940. Indeed, some say that Jackson had the best command of language of any Justice who has ever served on the Court. This from a Justice who never went to law school! The formidable Jackson was crucially aware of the importance of his performance as an oral advocate: "Over the years the time allotted for hearing has been shortened, but its importance has not diminished. The significance of the trend is that the shorter the time, the more precious is each minute."[37]

Theatrical presentations featuring soaring rhetoric simply do not occur before the modern Supreme Court. Such displays are actively discouraged. The Guide for Counsel that the Clerk of the Supreme Court issues to advocates contains the following advice for newcomers: "The Supreme Court is not a jury. A trial lawyer tries to persuade with facts and emotion. At this Court, counsel should try to persuade the Court by arguing legal theories."[38]

Reflecting the modern view of the purpose of oral argument, Justice Ruth Bader Ginsburg has noted, "Oral argument is an occasion not for grand speechmaking, but for an exchange of ideas about the case, a dialogue or discussion between knowledgeable counsel and judges who have done their homework. . . ."[39]

None of this is to say that oral arguments are boring. The arguments are engrossing to the lawyers, the parties, and the Justices. But modern oral arguments usually have rather limited appeal to the broader public, because the Court's modern practice has homed in on the legal, rather than the emotional, aspects of a case.

PERHAPS NO VIGNETTE BETTER captures the change in oral argument style than the showdown that occurred in the cases collectively known as *Brown v. Board of Education.* The case out of South Carolina featured John W. Davis arguing on behalf of a segregated school district against Thurgood Marshall arguing on behalf of the National Association for the Advancement of Colored People.

John Davis is often mentioned in the same breath as Webster as one of the most talented oral advocates to appear before the Court. Indeed, when Davis served as Solicitor General from 1913 to 1918, Chief Justice Charles Evans Hughes said that it was nothing less than "an intellectual treat" to hear Davis argue.[40] Justice Joseph Rucker Lamar went one step further and commented that Davis's persuasive argument style sometimes caused the Justices to stop posing queries. "John W. Davis has such a perfect flow of language," Justice Lamar said, "that we don't ask questions when we should."[41]

When Thurgood Marshall attended law school at Howard University, he would go to the Supreme Court to hear Davis argue. It would be difficult to exaggerate the esteem that Marshall felt for Davis. "I learned most of my stuff from him," Marshall said.[42] Marshall, who argued and won many cases before the Court, said of Davis: "He was a great advocate, the greatest."[43] "Every time John Davis argued," Marshall said, "I'd ask myself, 'Will I ever, ever . . . ?' and every time I had to answer, 'No. Never.' "[44]

With respect to their styles of presentation, Davis and Marshall were in marked contrast. Mark Tushnet, a professor at Harvard Law School, has described this difference: "Davis's oral arguments fit the public image of what oral advocacy could be. They were organized according to a rigid logic, had well-formed paragraphs that flowed easily into each other, and included the flowery eloquence characteristic of early twentieth century oratory."[45] Tushnet, who served as a law clerk to Marshall when he later became a Supreme Court Justice, noted that Marshall possessed a very different style of argumentation than Davis. "Marshall was able to capture the essence of his position in a phrase or two that established the common sense morality of his cause," Tushnet wrote, "but he did not hammer at that point. His style was almost conversational. When presenting the most far-reaching claims, Marshall's manner suggested that he and the Justices ought to talk about the problems the Justices might have, so that he and they could work them out as sensible people should."[46]

In the desegregation argument itself, which would be Davis's last before the Court, this stylistic contrast was on full display. "Mr. Davis was quite emotional," Chief Justice Earl Warren recollected. "In fact, he seemed to me to break down a few times during the hearing."[47] And Thurgood Marshall said that Davis's

This cartoon was drawn by Herbert Block ("Herblock") and inscribed to Chief Justice Earl Warren "To Chief Justice Warren / With affection and highest admiration / from Herb Block," in 1954, after the Brown v. Board decision.

cheeks were wet with tears as he returned to his seat following the conclusion of his case.

There is no case more important to this country's history than *Brown v. Board of Education,* of course, because it rejected the *Plessy* doctrine of "separate but equal" and promised the in-

The Supreme Court bench at the time of oral argument
in Grutter v. Bollinger.

tegration of black people, who had been treated as less than full citizens. But a smaller part of *Brown*'s legacy, one that has not received much attention, is the manner in which it illustrates the changing conception of what constitutes effective oral argument. Where Davis's lofty eloquence and emotional appeals once caused him to be regarded as the finest advocate of his time, Marshall's understated method of answering questions with succinct answers proved to be the path of the future.

AS THE STYLE OF ORAL advocacy has changed over time, it is hardly surprising that the style of questioning has also changed. Indeed, during arguments early in the Supreme Court's history, there were often no questions from the bench. In 1824, one newspaper correspondent described the Supreme Court as "not only one of the most dignified and enlightened tribunals in the world, but one of the most patient. Counsel are heard in silence for hours, without being stopped or interrupted."[48]

While I like to believe that the Court has retained both its dignity and its enlightenment, its reputation for patience is on shakier footing. Today, it is unusual for counsel to speak for more than a couple of minutes without being asked a question. Today's oral advocates must be skilled in navigating a barrage of questions, for they are likely to be peppered with them from the get-go.

In 1940, John Davis gave a famous address on oral argument to the New York Bar Association. In the speech, he handed down "Ten Commandments" to oral advocates:

1. Change places, in your imagination of course, with the Court.
2. State first the nature of the case and briefly its prior history.
3. State the facts.
4. State next the applicable rules of law on which you rely.
5. Always "go for the jugular vein."
6. Rejoice when the Court asks questions.
7. Read sparingly and only from necessity.
8. Avoid personalities.
9. Know your record from cover to cover.
10. Sit down.[49]

Of particular value is Davis's Sixth Commandment: "Rejoice when the Court asks questions." As Davis put it, "If the question does nothing more it gives you the assurance that the court is not comatose and that you have awakened at least a vestigial interest."[50]

Davis hit on an important point. If Justices do not frequently ask questions of the counsel before them, it is difficult to understand how the purpose of oral argument is distinct from the written briefs that lawyers submit ahead of argument. Oral argument is, among other things, an opportunity to press the advocates on points that the Justices regard as particularly difficult and requiring further elaboration. Oral argument is also an opportunity for counsel to respond to the Justices' concerns and explain why ruling in a client's favor is the most appropriate course of action. When the nine members of the Court gather for oral argument, it provides a chance for Justices to hear one another's concerns and views. This process is sometimes described as Justices having a conversation with one another, with the assistance of counsel.

Not only do Justices ask more questions, but the kinds of questions they pose have changed over time. E. Barrett Prettyman Jr., who was a law clerk at the Supreme Court during the 1950s, commented on the emergence of this trend: "There was a time, not many years ago, when a lawyer could feel reasonably confident as he approached oral argument in the United States Supreme Court if he had thoroughly absorbed the record in his case and had obtained a working knowledge of all relevant cases. No longer. Today, an advocate must, more than ever before, prepare himself for a stream of hypothetical questions touching not only on his own case but on a variety of unrelated facts and situations."[51] In the half century since Prettyman commented upon the increase in hypothetical questions, such questions have only increased.

This increase may be partly attributable to the number of Justices who were previously on law school faculties. Justices Ginsburg, Breyer, Scalia, and Kagan previously worked as full-time law professors. As Justice Ginsburg notes, "that breed is addicted to asking 'What if . . . , ' or 'Suppose that . . . .' "[52]

The rapid-fire questioning of oral argument can be overwhelming to advocates. In a 1944 case, *Hazel-Atlas Glass Co. v.*

Hartford-Empire Co., a lawyer fainted mid-argument. The case concerned the power of a court of appeals, when a successful litigant has committed a fraud on the court, to vacate its own judgment. The fraud allegations were supported by various affidavits and refuted by counter-affidavits. In the midst of discussing one particular affidavit, Justice William O. Douglas demanded of the oral advocate, "who drafted this affidavit?" The poor lawyer fell to the floor, hitting the table with his head in the process. His first action when he regained consciousness was to look straight at Justice Douglas and remark that "he had."[53]

MEMBERS OF THE COURT have expressed a wide range of opinions regarding the value of oral argument. On one end of the spectrum, Justice Oliver Wendell Holmes Jr. supposedly suggested to the Court's Reporter of decisions that his view of a case was never altered by oral argument.[54] On the opposite end of the spectrum, Justice William J. Brennan Jr. thought that oral argument was extremely important. "[O]ften my whole notion of what a case is about crystallizes at oral argument. . . . Oral argument with us is a Socratic dialogue between Justices and counsel."[55] During his stint on the U.S. Court of Appeals for the District of Columbia, Chief Justice John G. Roberts Jr. echoed Justice Brennan's sentiment, describing oral argument as a time "when ideas that have been percolating for some time begin to crystallize."[56]

For my part, I always found oral argument to be extremely helpful in shaping my views of a case. Often, I would enter oral argument with an inclination to vote in one direction or another, but I would continue to have some concerns about my final conclusion. Usually those concerns would be resolved by the end of the arguments.

People often ask me who the best oral advocate to argue before the Court was while I was on the bench. There were many talented oral advocates whom I heard, but no one presented better arguments on a more consistent basis than the current Chief Justice, John Roberts.

Roberts possessed an unusually clear and straightforward manner of presenting his arguments, even in cases that were highly technical or arcane. I understand that he refined this style by taking time to explain the gist of his cases to a person who was bright, but untrained in the law. I think that many other oral advocates would do well to take this page from Roberts's book.

Oral argument now is very different than it was in the early days of the Court. But one thing hasn't changed since the day when Chief Justice Marshall favored Pinkney with the highest possible praise. As Marshall recognized, a Justice's best work requires the clearheaded guidance of a brilliant oral advocate. Perhaps that legacy explains why Roberts had another tradition: Before arguing cases at the Supreme Court, Roberts would always touch the enormous statue of Chief Justice John Marshall that rests on the Supreme Court's ground floor. It is that connection between Justice and oral advocate that has remained constant from the inception of the Court.

CUSTOMS AND TRADITIONS
OF THE COURT

———⊹⊹———

A S THE SUPREME COURT HAS EVOLVED FROM ITS EARLY DAYS
to occupy a critical role in our democratic society, the
Justices have developed various customs and traditions.
Some are born of pragmatism or collegiality. Others are intended
to shape the manner in which the Court carries out its work.
Many of these public customs—those observed by visitors to the
Court—add formality and austerity to its proceedings and sym-
bolize the gravity of its role. On the other hand, most of the
Court's private customs—those observed only by the Justices—
reinforce the inherently intimate, collaborative nature of the
Justices' work and the importance of good relations among the
Justices to the successful completion of that work.

Perhaps the best-known rite of passage for each Supreme
Court Justice is the taking of the oath of office. An oath is constitutionally required of all federal employees, not just judges. Article VI, paragraph 3, the United States Constitution provides:

The Senators and Representatives before mentioned, and
the members of the several state legislatures, and all execu-

Supreme Court of the United States

No. ----- October Term, 1980

I, SANDRA DAY O'CONNOR, do solemnly swear that I
will support and defend the Constitution of the United States
against all enemies, foreign and domestic; that I will bear
true faith and allegiance to the same; that I take this
obligation freely, without any mental reservation or purpose
of evasion; and that I will well and faithfully discharge
the duties of the office on which I am about to enter.

So help me God.

Sandra Day O'Connor

Subscribed and sworn to before me this
twenty-fifth day of September, 1981

Warren E. Burger

Chief Justice of the United States

*Justice Sandra Day O'Connor's Judicial Oath of Office, signed by O'Connor
and witnessed by Chief Justice Warren E. Burger.*

tive and judicial officers, both of the United States and of the several states, shall be bound by oath or affirmation, to support this Constitution; but no religious test shall ever be required as a qualification to any office or public trust under the United States.

The wording of the oath, however, was left up to Congress. The original version of the Constitutional Oath, used from 1789 to 1861, read: "I do solemnly swear (or affirm) that I will support the Constitution of the United States." Starting in the middle of the nineteenth century, the oath was changed several times before Congress settled on the version used today. Codified by statute, the oath now reads:

> I, _____, do solemnly swear (or affirm) that I will support and defend the Constitution of the United States against all enemies, foreign and domestic; that I will bear true faith and allegiance to the same; that I take this obligation freely, without any mental reservation or purpose of evasion; and that I will well and faithfully discharge the duties of the office on which I am about to enter. So help me God.[1]

The Constitutional Oath is now taken by all federal employees, except the President.[2]

In addition to the Constitutional Oath, Congress established a Judicial Oath. The requirement that all judges take this oath was set out in the Judiciary Act of 1789, which required that "the justices of the Supreme Court, and the district judges, before they proceed to execute the duties of their respective offices" take an oath or affirmation. As revised by the Judicial Improvements Act of 1990, the Judicial Oath now reads:

> I, _____, do solemnly swear (or affirm) that I will ad-

minister justice without respect to persons, and do equal right to the poor and to the rich, and that I will faithfully and impartially discharge and perform all the duties incumbent upon me as _____ under the Constitution and laws of the United States. So help me God.[3]

Justice Clarence Thomas became the first Justice to take the revised oath, in October 1991, and every Justice confirmed since has followed suit.

If two oaths are too many, a Justice can instead swear the Combined Oath. It reads:

I, _____, do solemnly swear (or affirm) that I will administer justice without respect to persons, and do equal right to the poor and to the rich, and that I will faithfully and impartially discharge and perform all the duties incumbent upon me as _____ under the Constitution and laws of the United States; and that I will support and defend the Constitution of the United States against all enemies, foreign and domestic; that I will bear true faith and allegiance to the same; that I take this obligation freely, without any mental reservation or purpose of evasion; and that I will well and faithfully discharge the duties of the office on which I am about to enter. So help me God.[4]

Chief Justice Earl Warren chose the Combined Oath after receiving his permanent commission when he was sworn in on March 20, 1954. President Eisenhower had appointed Warren five months earlier during a congressional recess after the death of Chief Justice Fred Vinson. Warren had already taken each oath separately for his recess appointment, so he was perhaps tired of oaths by the time the Senate ratified his permanent appointment. On June 23, 1969, he administered the Combined Oath in open Court to his successor, Chief Justice Warren Burger. This was the first time an outgoing chief swore in his replacement, and Chief Justice Burger perhaps thus saw fit to use the same oath his predecessor had sworn.

NEITHER ARTICLE VI OF the Constitution nor federal statutes specify a procedure for taking the oaths. The first Chief Justice, John Jay, took both of his oaths from the Chief Justice of New York, Richard Morris, in an unremarkable ceremony in a state courtroom on October 19, 1789. [5] He wasn't even the first Justice to do so; two weeks earlier, Justice James Wilson had claimed the honor of becoming the first fully vested member of the Court by taking his oaths. There was no requirement that the oath be taken before another judge, so Justice Wilson had taken his oaths before the mayor of Philadelphia.[6]

After the establishment of the federal circuit courts, Justices typically took their oaths either upon receipt of their commission or when they arrived at the circuit courts to perform their circuit justice duties.[7] Due to the magnitude of their circuit responsibilities, Justices were more likely to arrive at a circuit court before they arrived for a sitting of the Supreme Court. When Justices arrived to sit with the Supreme Court for the first time, if they had already taken the oaths at the circuit court, they would "present [their] commission[s] to the Clerk of the Court who would read it aloud in open court and record it in the Court's minutes."[8]

In the second half of the 1800s, the Supreme Court Term increased in length. Around that time, the Justices' circuit court duties also decreased, such that new Justices were more likely to arrive first to the Supreme Court before they embarked upon circuit responsibilities.[9] At that time, a tradition began of having two oath ceremonies. The first ceremony involved the Constitutional Oath—the one given to all federal employees. That ceremony was usually held in private at the Supreme Court, and the Chief Justice or Senior Associate Justice administered the Constitutional Oath to the new Justice.[10] The second ceremony was a public one in which the Clerk of the Court administered the Judicial Oath.[11]

The tradition of two ceremonies has been followed since the late 1800s, but the location of the Constitutional Oath ceremony

Harlan Fiske Stone being sworn in as Chief Justice
at Rocky Mountain National Park.

has varied. In 1940, President Franklin D. Roosevelt invited newly appointed Justice Frank Murphy to take his Constitutional Oath in a ceremony at the White House.[12] Justices since that time have usually taken an oath at the White House, though sometimes they were retaking an oath for the White House ceremony because they had already taken both oaths at an earlier time. For example, Justice Anthony Kennedy took both oaths in the Justices' Conference Room at the Supreme Court on February 18, 1988, took the Judicial Oath again in open court during a special sitting on the same day, and took the Constitutional Oath again the next day at a special White House ceremony with President Reagan.[13] Recently, some Justices have voiced concerns about this trend. Justice John Paul Stevens, for instance, has expressed a preference for holding the ceremony at the Supreme Court rather than the White House to better symbolize the separation of powers among the three branches of government and underscore the independence of the judiciary.[14]

At other times, special circumstances have caused Justices to take the oaths in unconventional locations. For example, Chief Justice Harlan Fiske Stone was confirmed in July 1941 while he was on vacation in Colorado. Chief Justice Stone received a telegram from the White House informing him of his confirmation, and then took both the Constitutional and Judicial oaths at the Sprague Hotel in Colorado before the U.S. commissioner for Rocky Mountain National Park, Wayne H. Hackett.[15] In the summer of 1994, newly confirmed Justice Stephen Breyer was so eager to get a start on his new duties that he traveled all the way to Chief Justice Rehnquist's rustic summer cottage on the shores of Caspian Lake in northeastern Vermont for a swearing-in ceremony with just his wife at his side, without the knowledge of the press. Justice Breyer's secretary had told a reporter that morning that the Justice was merely out running errands, and the Supreme Court's public information officer did not inform reporters about the ceremony until an hour after it had occurred.[16]

Of course, with so many oaths come many great firsts. For example, when President Franklin D. Roosevelt invited Justice Murphy to take his Constitutional Oath at the White House on January 18, 1940, he became the first President to witness a Justice's oath, and Murphy became the first Justice sworn in at the White House. On October 1, 1945, President Harry S. Truman became the first President to visit the Supreme Court for an oath ceremony when he witnessed Justice Harold H. Burton taking the Judicial Oath in the courtroom.

Justice Antonin Scalia can claim a unique accomplishment. He was the first Justice to take his oaths from different Chief Justices on the same day. On September 26, 1986, retiring Chief Justice Warren E. Burger administered Justice Scalia's Constitutional Oath at the White House, where he also administered that oath to the new Chief, William Rehnquist. Later that day, Chief Justice Burger administered the Judicial Oath to Rehnquist at

Swearing-in ceremony for Chief Justice William H. Rehnquist and Justice Antonin Scalia, which took place in the East Room of the White House on September 26, 1986.

the Court. The new Chief Justice Rehnquist then administered the Judicial Oath to Justice Scalia.[17]

Not to be outdone, Justice David Souter was the first to take an oath on national television. On October 8, 1990, President George H. W. Bush looked on at the White House as Chief Justice Rehnquist administered Justice Souter's Constitutional Oath before the cameras.

Before taking his seat at the center of the Court's bench for the first time, the Court's current Chief Justice, John G. Roberts Jr., took part in a series of oath-taking ceremonies. On September 29, 2005, Justice Stevens administered the Judicial Oath to the new Chief in a private, intimate ceremony in the diplomatic reception room at the White House, attended by the Chief's family and other members of the Supreme Court. Later that day, Justice Stevens administered the Constitutional Oath to the Chief Justice in a public ceremony at the White House that was attended by President George W. Bush and broadcast worldwide on live television. Other members of the Supreme Court, their spouses, and many dignitaries also attended this ceremony. And Chief Justice Roberts was still not finished swearing oaths when he left the White House. A week later, he was again sworn in, this time in a private investiture ceremony for the Chief Justice in the courtroom, one hour before the Court's Term began on the first Monday in October 2005.

The two newest Justices, Justice Sonia Sotomayor and Justice Elena Kagan, did not take either of their oaths at the White House. Both took their Constitutional Oath in the Justices' Conference Room at the Supreme Court, in front of family, friends, and other Justices, and then their Judicial Oath in one of the Supreme Court conference rooms, before a small gathering of family and friends. Both of their Judicial Oath ceremonies were broadcast live on television.[18] Each later retook the Judicial Oath in a formal investiture ceremony in the Supreme Court's courtroom with President Barack Obama in attendance.[19] No photo-

Justice Sandra Day O'Connor signing her oaths of office in the Justices' Conference Room as Chief Justice Warren E. Burger looks on, September 25, 1981.

graphs or videos are permitted in the Court courtroom, so there are no photos of the formal investiture ceremonies. The iconic photos of new Justices usually come from the moments after the ceremony when the Chief Justice and the new Justice walk down the grand white marble steps in front of the Court to greet reporters gathered on the Supreme Court plaza. Only the Justices know what they and the Chief Justice discuss while they walk down the steps to the flash of hundreds of cameras.

As the first woman appointed to the Court, I was naturally the first woman Justice to take the oaths. I was also the first to have guests in the Justice's private conference room to watch the ceremony. On September 25, 1981, I took my oath in that intimate setting, joined by my husband, President Ronald Reagan, Mrs. Nancy Reagan, and Mrs. Vera Burger, wife of Chief Justice Warren Burger. It was an incredibly special moment, one I will never forget.

One interesting feature of the formal investiture ceremonies is

*Justice O'Connor with Chief Justice Burger and President Reagan
the day of her investiture, 1981.*

that since Lewis Powell's ceremony in 1972, each newly appointed Justice is permitted to sit in the historic chair used by Chief Justice John Marshall.[20] The chair sits at the well of the courtroom below the bench and has been well preserved, but needless to say, its use is reserved for this very special occasion. Justice Sotomayor recently called sitting in the ceremonial chair the "most symbolically meaningful moment" of her investiture, saying she felt as if emotion and "history [were] coursing through" her.[21] I myself vividly remember being escorted to that chair by Alexander Stevas, the Supreme Court chief clerk, on September 25, 1981, while my husband, three sons, mother, father, sister, and brother looked on. It was also the first of many Supreme Court traditions I would have the honor of experiencing as a Justice. Indeed, customs pervade the day-to-day work of a Justice.

ONE OF MY FAVORITE traditions—the judicial handshake—takes place just before oral argument. Before taking the bench, as we

The bench chair used by Chief Justice John Marshall, roughly 1819–1835. It is the only piece of furniture known to survive from the set made for the Court's use in 1819.

say, the Justices gather in the robing room and each Justice shakes hands with and greets every other Justice—thirty-six handshakes in all. Although there is some dispute, the prevailing view is that the custom was instituted by Chief Justice Melville

Fuller, who served as chief from 1888 until 1910. Known as "the judicial handshake" even though there are many handshakes involved, the custom is meant to symbolize that the Justices must all work together regardless of personal or ideological differences. It ensures that the frustrations and rancor that are too often the result of passionate disagreement are cast aside, or sufficiently quelled, to allow for a cordial greeting before every session of the Court. It reminds each Justice, moments before taking the bench, that the work of the Court is by necessity collaborative and is carried out by an intimate group of colleagues and friends.

I have vivid memories of the first judicial handshake I experienced. That was mostly due to Justice Byron White, an NFL football star who possessed, as I soon learned the hard way, a viselike grip. As I shook each of my new colleagues' hands, Justice Byron White shook my hand in his with such force that I felt tears spring to my eyes from the pain! From then on, I resolved to grab his thumb instead of giving him my hand. That was a preemptive measure I knew I needed to take to endure the many handshakes to come in the years ahead!

When the Justices finish shaking hands, two more customs stand between them and their seats. The first governs the manner in which they dramatically enter the courtroom. Four grand columns stand behind the bench, creating three spaces through which the Justices can enter. Elegant drapes create a narrow entrance in each of those spaces. The three entrances are equally shared by the nine Justices; three Justices enter through each entrance.

The Court's marshal simultaneously carries out the final custom in a ceremony that is as well choreographed as it is brief. The Justices' entrance is heralded by the marshal's loud bang of her gavel, which signals all present in the courtroom to stand. As the Justices next emerge in their triple trios, the marshal declares in a booming voice: "The Honorable, the Chief Justice, and the Associate Justices of the Supreme Court of the United States." When the Justices reach their seats, she continues: "Oyez! Oyez! Oyez! All persons having business before the Honorable, the Supreme Court of the United States, are admonished to draw near and give their attention, for the Court is now sitting. God save the United States and this Honorable Court." A second rap of her gavel ends the proclamation and everyone sits.

The Justices' practice of entering the courtroom in three groups of three began when the Supreme Court moved to its present home in 1937. However, the opening cry was instituted much earlier. On February 2, 1790, with a quorum of four of the six Justices present, a simple announcement for silence marked the start of the Court's proceedings at the Merchants Exchange Building in New York City. The newly formed Court appointed its first "cryer," Richard Wenman. The next day, Wenman cried the Court for the first time. The cry has been heard before every sitting since, though the text has varied slightly over the years. The cryer did not fare as well as the cry. After approximately thirty people held this ceremonial post, it was eliminated in 1962. The Court's marshal has assumed the duty of delivering the Court's invocation ever since.

When morning arguments conclude, the Justices gather for another tradition, one less formal and more necessary: lunch. Each day during which the Court hears argument, the Justices convene in the Justices' dining room at approximately noon to share a meal and conversation. By rule, the work of the Court is not to be discussed. The meal is meant to be a respite from the intense pace of the Court's business and an opportunity for colleagues and friends to reconnect. In keeping with this informality, Justices do not sit in order of seniority during lunch. However, another custom governs the seating chart. Upon joining the Court, each Justice is assigned the lunch seat of the Justice he or she replaced. In this way, a Justice's perspective is passed on from successor to successor—his perspective of the dining room.

* * *

LUNCH ASIDE, BY LONG-standing tradition the principle of judicial seniority plays an active role in the organization and operation of the Supreme Court and, indeed, the entire federal judiciary. Thus, when the Justices sit on the bench, they do so in order of seniority, with the Chief Justice at the center, presiding over the Court's proceedings. The Justices are similarly organized by seniority in virtually all of the public ceremonies in which they participate.

The seniority system has important, substantive impacts on the Court's business. For example, it is the most senior Justice in the majority who assigns the responsibility of writing an opinion for the Court. Similarly, when the Justices meet in private conference to discuss cases, their seniority dictates the order in which they comment and vote on the cases before the Court. Seniority confers greater stature in public rituals and the opportunity for greater influence over the Court's work.

Conversely, by tradition the Court's most junior Justice inherits a range of duties that might fittingly be described as undesirable. For example, the Justices depart the courtroom in order of seniority, leaving the junior Justice at the rear. He or she is also the last in line to enter when Justices attend the President's annual State of the Union address, presidential inaugurations, and other ceremonies. Most notably, the junior Justice serves as the link between the confidential world of the Conference—attended only by the nine sitting members of the Court—and the world of the Court beyond the conference room walls. The two most significant duties associated with this role are answering the door when Court personnel knock and delivering outgoing messages from the Justices to attendants waiting beyond the door.

When I was confirmed, I replaced Justice Stevens as the most junior Justice on the Court. There was some discussion, I learned, over whether I would be offended as a woman by being delegated

Justices at President Clinton's State of the Union Address in January 1998.

such unglamorous duties. There need not have been any concern, however. Justice Stevens reportedly spoke up and stated that he believed I would not want to be treated differently from any other Justice. He was right, of course. I was more than happy to continue the tradition. I served as the doorkeeper for five years until Justice Scalia's appointment to the Court in 1986 ultimately gave me a reprieve, as he assumed those duties.

The most junior Justice also has the responsibility of serving on the Court's cafeteria committee. In this capacity, Justice Kagan, currently the most junior Justice on the Court, recently introduced frozen yogurt and pretzels to the Supreme Court cafeteria.

THESE MYRIAD CUSTOMS OFFER insight into how the Court has evolved from its early days as a neglected institution with little work and no home. The Supreme Court is a tradition-bound institution—and its many traditions shape both the Court's day-to-day operations and its broader role in our society.

SOME LAUGHS ON THE BENCH

———————//———————

THE CORRIDORS AND CHAMBERS AT THE SUPREME COURT ARE usually exceedingly quiet. Justice Oliver Wendell Holmes Jr. once wrote that the Court has "the quiet of a storm center."[1] The Court's chambers are occupied by the Justices and their law clerks, all of them reading and doing research about difficult issues in cases they are trying to resolve. Nevertheless, the studious and serious environment at the Court is punctuated by humor and the occasional jest. All of us enjoy a good joke and a hearty laugh—and Supreme Court Justices are no exception.

SOMETIMES THE LAUGHS TAKE place in the courtroom during the rapid-fire exchanges of oral argument. In 2005, one law professor combed through the seventy-five oral argument transcripts from the October 2004 Term. The professor set about "calculat[ing] each Justice's 'Laughter Episodes Instigated Per Argument Average,' or LEIPAA, which represents the total number of laughter episodes instigated over the term divided by the number of oral arguments attended over the course of the term."[2]

What were his findings? Justice Antonin Scalia apparently "won the competition by a landslide," generating seventy-seven LEIPAAs that year.[3] He was followed by Justice Stephen Breyer with forty-five instances of laughter. It appears that I came in short at seventh place!

The New York Times did a humorous piece on the "study" designating Justice Scalia the title of "funniest Justice."[4] Justice Ruth Bader Ginsburg has said that on certain occasions Justice Scalia would "say something that was so outrageous or so funny that I had to pinch myself so I wouldn't laugh out loud in the courtroom."[5]

Justice Scalia's chief competitor for the title of "funniest Justice," Justice Breyer, drew particularly "raucous laughter and howls" for a remark he made in a Fourth Amendment case. The issue before the Court involved an intrusive search of a student conducted by school officials who suspected that the student was carrying drugs in her clothes.[6] The oral argument saw the Jus-

Justice O'Connor chats with Justice Breyer prior to
President George W. Bush's first inauguration, in 2001.

tices grappling with the difficult issue of whether the search was justified.

In the midst of the argument, Justice Breyer remarked: "In my experience when I was eight or ten or twelve years old, you know, we did take our clothes off once a day, we changed for gym, okay? And in my experience, too, people did sometimes stick things in my underwear—"

Flustered by the ensuing laughter, Justice Breyer quickly retracted: "Or not my underwear. Whatever. Whatever. I was the one who did it? I don't know."

Even our current Chief Justice, John G. Roberts Jr., has garnered attention for his "light, witty touch" at oral argument.[7] Chief Justice Roberts presided over one of his first oral argument sessions on October 31, 2005, which fell on Halloween. It was a difficult case on state sovereign immunity in the bankruptcy context. Suddenly, a lightbulb exploded above the Justices in the middle of a comment by Justice Ginsburg.

"I think we're . . . I think it's safe. It's a trick they play on new chief justices all the time," the Chief joked.

"Happy Halloween," replied Justice Scalia.

"We're even more in the dark now than before," the Chief Justice deadpanned. Justice Ginsburg nonetheless proceeded with her comment as if nothing had happened.

The attention to the Justices' sense of humor has even extended to the judicial confirmation process. During the confirmation hearings for Elena Kagan, Senator Charles Schumer of New York touted Justice Kagan's potential in this regard. Noting that "Justice Scalia gets the most laughs," he praised the nominee: "If you get there, and I believe you will, you're going to give him a run for his money."[8]

Some of the jokes at oral argument come from the advocates themselves. Such attempts at humor can hit or miss. In the famous abortion case *Roe v. Wade,* defendant Henry Wade's lawyer, an assistant attorney general from the state of Texas, opened his argument with a joke that fell flat. He began: "Mr. Chief Justice and may it please the Court. It's an old joke, but when a man argues against two beautiful ladies like this, they are going to have the last word." The courtroom remained silent, a cool reminder that cracking jokes during argument can be a precarious endeavor.[9] I'm sure that lawyer thought twice before attempting another joke at his next argument.

ONE FREQUENT—AND INADVERTENT—source of hilarity during oral argument arises when advocates, while fielding tough questions from the panel of nine Justices, mix up the Justices. Poor Justice Souter was called the wrong name on several occasions. At an argument in 2004, one of my former law clerks, Sri Srinivasan, argued before the Court on behalf of the United States. Sri accidentally referred to Justice Souter as "Justice Scalia" and quickly apologized. Souter did not miss a beat and responded, "Thank you, but apologize to him." In 2007, a lawyer again referred to Souter by the wrong name—this time, as "Justice Ginsburg." Souter replied, again with unflappable calm, "I'm Justice Souter. . . . You're very flattering."[10]

It seems that the mix-ups plagued Justice Souter even outside the Supreme Court. Justice Breyer and his wife, Joanna, were at their cabin in New Hampshire one year. A fellow pulled over in a pickup with a rifle on a rack in the truck and asked to talk to the Justice about "what's going on in Washington about guns." After Justice Breyer informed the man that it would be better to send any information to him by mail, the man thanked him: "Good to meet you, Justice Souter." When Souter heard the story, he said that it could only have happened in his home state of New Hampshire. Soon afterward, however, Souter found himself in Massachusetts. A man on the street approached to shake his hand, exclaiming, "Mom, Mom, come over and shake hands with Justice Breyer. You know, he's the one from New Hampshire, the one you like!"

In another incident, Justice Souter was having dinner in Massachusetts when someone approached him to ask how he was enjoying his "first year" on the Supreme Court. When Souter realized that he was being confused with Justice Breyer, who had taught at Harvard Law School and served as a federal judge in Boston, he decided to play along so as not to embarrass the stranger. The best thing about his year on the Court, he said, "was getting to know David Souter. He's one heck of a guy."

INDEED, PEOPLE SOMETIMES FORGET that the Justices are good friends as well as professional colleagues—and every friendship endures the occasional ribbing. Even Justice Story once joked about Chief Justice Marshall's penchant for wine. In an interview with Josiah Quincy about the Court, Justice Story reportedly quipped:

> [The Justices'] intercourse is perfectly familiar and unrestrained, and our social hours, when undisturbed with the labors of law, are passed in gay and frank conversation. . . . We are great ascetics, and even deny ourselves wine, except in wet weather. What I say about the wine, sir, gives you our rule: but it does sometimes happen that the Chief Justice will say to me, when the cloth is removed, "Brother Story, step to the window and see if it does not look like rain." And if I tell him in reply that the sun is shining brightly, Justice Marshall will sometimes reply, "all the better; for our jurisdiction extends over so large a territory that the doctrine of chances makes it certain that it must be raining somewhere." You know that the Chief was brought up on Federalism and Madeira, and he is not the man to outgrow his early prejudices.[11]

Meanwhile, Justice Harry Blackmun had some fun at Justice William O. Douglas's expense during the Vietnam War. Douglas was convinced that FBI director J. Edgar Hoover had installed some kind of eavesdropping device in the Court's Conference Room and he repeatedly called for having the room swept for the presence of electronic bugs. The other Justices brushed him off as a little paranoid, until one day when they heard a high-pitched electronic beep coming from someplace in the room. Justice Douglas slammed one hand down on the table and said he had known it all along; the sound was obviously coming from a malfunctioning bug planted somewhere in the room, and now maybe they'd agree that the place had to be swept. He had his way, and the premises got a meticulous examination. But no bug or electronic irregularity turned up. When the result was reported, Justice Blackmun was seen to be smiling quietly, as the hand cradling his head touched the hearing aid placed unobtrusively in his ear. After my arrival at the Court in 1981, I too remember hearing the faint noises of Blackmun's hearing aid during Conference and wondering what the sounds were. By that time, I suppose, my colleagues had gotten used to it.

Justice Hugo Black once poked fun at Chief Justice Warren Burger's eagerness to improve the lighting in the Justices' chambers. The Chief apparently thought there would be no enthusiasm for the change unless he could provide a convincing demonstration of more effective lighting. During one of the Court's longer breaks between weeks of oral arguments, the Chief Justice had fluorescent lighting panels installed in the ceilings of his own chambers and in the Justices' Conference Room. With the new light panels in place, he invited the other Justices to come in and admire the display. The story I heard was that Justice Black duly appeared, said nothing, and looked at Chief Justice Burger's expectant face as he prepared to leave. Justice Black's head shook slightly and he spoke in an exaggerated, quavering voice. "Oh, Mr. Chief Justice," said the man who had once told President Harry Truman to take his hands off the nation's steel mills, and who had stopped President Nixon's attempt to suppress the Pentagon Papers, "a-a-all these changes . . . a-a-all these changes!"

As a Supreme Court Justice, you spend a lot of time with the same eight people over the years. When I announced my intent to retire in 2005, the composition of the Court had not changed for eleven years. Over those years, I certainly got well-acquainted with the lighter side of my colleagues. I often think of Justice Thurgood Marshall's very good sense of humor. He was a fine raconteur. He once told me a story about meeting Britain's Prince Philip in Kenya during the celebrations after Jomo Kenyatta's inauguration as prime minister in 1963. Prince Philip asked him, in his highbrow British accent, "And what do you do?" Justice Marshall responded that he was a lawyer. Prince Philip mumbled, "Hmph," which the Justice took as mild disapproval. Justice Marshall immediately responded, "Would you like to know what I think of princes?" At that witty reply, Prince Philip smiled broadly and said, "Not at all. Let's go have a drink."

While Justice Marshall's sense of humor was widely known, I have found that few people know of how amusing Chief Justice Bill Rehnquist could be. Many people did not know of his relaxed side and his penchant for spoofs, skits, and contests of all stripes.[12] There are some comical photographs of him from his days as a law clerk at the Court in 1952—smoking and drinking at his desk and delivering remarks as his fellow clerk C. George Niebank Jr. pretended to worship a fountain in one of the Supreme Court courtyards.[13] A Gilbert & Sullivan aficionado, Chief Justice Rehnquist once composed a spoof of the opera *The Mikado* for his former boss, Justice Robert Jackson. The spoof included such lyrics as:

Now Stanley Reed evades the ban
In about the only way he can

"Without a label
No one is able
To tell if I'm dissenting"[14]

That was a tweak at Justice Stanley Reed, who reportedly had a reputation, whether fair or unfair, for opinions that did not make clear whether they reflected, concurred, or dissented from the judgment of the Court.

Chief Justice Rehnquist's penchant for music even made its way into the Court's internal communications. On one occasion, the Chief circulated a draft opinion in *Barnes v. Glen Theatre, Inc.,* a landmark decision from 1991 on whether nude dancing was protected under the First Amendment. The Chief enclosed a cover memorandum to me and the other Justices quoting from Johnny Mercer's popular song, "Ac-cent-tchu-ate the Positive," which topped the charts in 1945. His memorandum expressed his hope that the theme of his draft was a "very positive one" that could be summed up as follows: "Accentuate the positive / Eliminate the negative / Latch on to the affirmative / Don't mess with Mr. In Between."[15]

Always a prankster, Rehnquist once played an elaborate April Fool's Day joke on his predecessor as Chief Justice, Warren Burger. He had a street photographer offer tourists the opportunity to be photographed with a life-size cutout of Burger, and rode to Court that day with the enormous photograph, just to make sure Burger caught wind of the prank.[16]

It seems that Rehnquist liked to poke fun at former Chief Justices. At a 1992 ceremony celebrating the issuance of a postal stamp picturing former Chief Justice Earl Warren, Rehnquist declared dryly, "Earl Warren was of Scandinavian descent on both sides of his family—his father immigrated from Norway and his mother immigrated from Sweden. I like to think of him as the first of the great Scandinavian-American Chief Justices."[17]

In fact, Rehnquist was the driving force behind one tradition that today remains a great source of entertainment at the Court—the "parody" that the law clerks put on for the Justices and staff at the end of each Term. As a new Justice, Rehnquist urged Chief Justice Burger to institute the annual show. Rehnquist even attempted to persuade the Supreme Court press corps to put on a show for the Justices as well, though without success.[18] One journalist reportedly told him, "We don't mind eating your food and drinking your wine, but we're not trained monkeys."[19] The law clerks, however, obliged, and now every year, the law clerks lampoon the Justices and events of the Term. I distinctly recall the parody in 1994, when the movie *Jurassic Park* had been the previous summer's blockbuster. Harry Blackmun, as played by a law clerk in the skit, exclaimed in one scene, "Dinosaurs! Yes, I remember dinosaurs. Warren [Burger] and I used to ride them when we were boys!"

SERIOUS AND STRESSFUL THOUGH the job can be, it has always been important to the Justices that the law clerks enjoy a social and collegial environment. Another tradition has been for the law clerks to let loose at weekly basketball games in the Supreme Court's gymnasium, located directly above the courtroom and affectionately known as the "highest court in the land." Justice Byron White was known for joining the clerks for the afternoon games. To be sure, it was wonderful of Justice White to take the time to get to know some of the law clerks better. But Justice White also had a fierce competitive streak. One day, Justice White swung his arm back and accidentally hit the Adam's apple of a hapless young clerk, who collapsed and passed out. White picked him up, looked at him, and said, "You're all right, aren't you?" "Yes, sir," came the feeble response, to which White said, "Well, then get on with the game!"

Some years later, Justice Thomas, who also took to the basketball court on occasion, broke a leg. He walked around in a cast.

Justices at President Bill Clinton's second inauguration, in 1997.

When Justice Kennedy asked Justice White, "Byron, did you do that to him?" Justice White disclaimed responsibility: "If it had been me, both his legs would have been in a cast."

A sense of humor is a valuable commodity in any occupation, and it certainly is appreciated in the hallowed halls of the Supreme Court of the United States.

LARGER-THAN-LIFE JUSTICES

—————//—————

I F YOU VISIT THE GROUND FLOOR OF THE SUPREME COURT BUILD-
ing, you will find the halls adorned with a bit of art—mostly
portraits of departed associate justices. Many of the portraits
you will find there are unfamiliar—all of them men, who have
served the country on the Court, usually with honor, but whom
history has all but forgotten. Others, however, are unforgettable.
In this chapter are written "portraits" of four Justices who were
larger-than-life: Justices Stephen Field, Oliver Wendell Holmes
Jr., James McReynolds, and William O. Douglas.

These are not necessarily the greatest *jurists* the Court has
known, though Holmes certainly falls in that category. Instead,
they are men whose *personalities* were so big that they have made
their mark on history by sheer force of character. And the character of at least one of them may seem more shadow than light.
But whatever judgment history has passed on them, it is worth
knowing about each of these men.

They came from the Northeast, the South, and the far West,
and their tenures on the Court spanned the century from the
Civil War to the Vietnam War. Each was shaped by, and shaped,

Formal half-length portrait photograph of Justice Stephen J. Field in his robes, circa 1890.

his times and circumstances. And each reveals that the judge is more than his jurisprudence. Underneath their robes, so to speak, the Justices of the Supreme Court are real, often quite unique, people. With all the current focus on judges' so-called ideologies, it is worth remembering that a judge's personal history and character also matter—for they can do a great deal to enrich or impoverish our courts.

JUSTICE STEPHEN J. FIELD was a genuine pioneer. His rise to the Supreme Court began with the gold rush of 1849. That year, at the age of thirty-three, Field left his legal practice in New York City to make his fortune in California. Within a year of his arrival in the Golden State, Field had helped to establish the frontier town of Marysville, near the gold fields in the foothills of the Sierra Nevada. He was soon elected justice of the peace, and it was during his brief tenure in that office that he got his first taste of judging.

One account tells how Field presided over a trial involving a dispute about rights to a mining claim. For lack of a courtroom, the trial was held in a local saloon and gambling house. After the jury ruled for the plaintiff, the lawyer for the defendants denounced the jury and said that he would "advise his Clients to resist that verdict at the point of the knife and the knife to the hilt." The jury foreman drew a pistol, but Field intervened. Field reportedly took a bowie knife from his pocket and placed it between his teeth, then drew a pistol and placed it within six inches of the offending lawyer's head. "Eat those words, damn you, or I'll send you to hell," Fields said, and the offending counsel gulped and said, "I eat." With that, court was adjourned.[1] The tale may be tall, but the portrait of frontier justice rings true.

Field was soon elected to a term in the California Assembly, but the state legislature wasn't much more civilized than Field's bar-side courtroom. Field later recounted that more than two-thirds of the thirty-six assemblymen *never* appeared unarmed, and that it was not unheard-of for a legislator to brandish a pistol to emphasize a point in debate. In 1857, Field was elected to the three-member California Supreme Court, where he served for six years. But even here, violence was never distant. David S. Terry, one of Field's fellow justices and a lifelong nemesis, was forced to step down after shooting a leading political adversary to death in a duel.

In 1863, Congress expanded the number of Justices on the U.S. Supreme Court to ten. President Lincoln nominated Field to the tenth seat, informally designated for a representative of the western states. In 1869 Congress returned the Court to its present size of nine. But Field remained on the Court and served for a remarkable thirty-four years, stepping down at last in 1897.

Field's jurisprudence marked him as a friend of business, an opponent of expansive federal regulation, and a strong advocate of states' rights. He pioneered the notion that the Due Process Clause of the Fourteenth Amendment provides a substantive restriction on government regulation of business, and that the Constitution protects liberty of contract and the right to pursue one's trade. For instance, Field disagreed with the majority of the Court in a decision upholding the Illinois legislature's right to fix maximum storage rates charged by grain elevators and public warehouses and to require licenses to operate such facilities. Writing in dissent, Field declared: "I deny the power of any legislature under our government to fix the price which anyone shall receive for his property of any kind."[2] "If the power can be exercised as to one article," he warned, "it may as to all articles, and the prices of every thing, from a calico gown to a city mansion, may be subject to legislative direction."[3] Although he advocated these principles most often in dissent, ironically his views came to prevail almost immediately after his retirement. For the first four decades of the twentieth century, the theory of economic rights Field pioneered held sway in the nation's high court, as the Court invalidated various federal and state laws that regulated business and labor.

During his tenure on the Court, Field twice ran for President of the United States—in 1880 and 1884. In those days it was not unprecedented for a sitting Justice to run for political office, but it was still unusual. And there is little question that Field's political aspirations influenced to a degree his performance on the bench. He actively used his pro–states' rights opinions in civil rights cases, for example, to seek voter support in the South.

Though Field found a place in the national political limelight, he never lost touch with his roots in California. During that era, Supreme Court Justices were still required to leave Washington, D.C., each year to ride circuit—that is, to sit with other judges on the lower federal courts in the region to which the Justice was assigned. Justice Field was assigned to the Ninth Circuit, which, as now, encompassed California and the rest of the far West. He logged thousands upon thousands of miles of travel each year to attend these duties. In 1889, a remarkable thing happened to Field while riding circuit.

Four years earlier, Field had participated in a case in which Field's old rival and former fellow California Supreme Court justice, David S. Terry, represented one of the parties. Field had sent Terry to jail for six months for contempt of court, and Terry publicly threatened retaliation. Four years later, while Field was riding circuit in California, Terry boarded the train on which Field was traveling. An altercation ensued, and Field's bodyguard shot Terry dead. Both the bodyguard and Field were arrested, though they were ultimately released. Frontier justice, it seemed, had followed Stephen Field all the way to the Supreme Court of the United States.

In 1902, five years after Justice Field's retirement, Oliver Wendell Holmes Jr. was appointed to the Supreme Court. Holmes was born the son of a prominent family in Cambridge, Massachusetts, far from the California gold fields. He grew up a "Boston Brahmin" who kept company with Ralph Waldo Emerson and other intellectual notables. Indeed, his father was himself a noted writer and physician. Holmes had his intellectual formation in the halls of Harvard and the Boston salons, and was one of the most erudite men ever to sit on the Supreme Court. But perhaps the most formative experience of Holmes's early life was his service as an officer in the Union army during the Civil War. Holmes was seriously wounded four separate times during the course of the war, and scores of his close friends from Boston were killed. He saw death on a gruesome scale and returned from the war with a deep sense of skepticism about human nature and the existence of firm truths. Yet he also retained an intense and virile passion for life.

Much later in life Holmes gave a speech titled "The Soldier's Faith," which seemed to describe the war's ambivalent imprint on him. He said: "I do not know what is true. I do not know the meaning of the universe. But in the midst of doubt, in the collapse of creeds, there is one thing I do not doubt, and that is that the faith is true . . . which leads a soldier to throw away his life in obedience to a blindly accepted duty, in a cause which he little understands, in a plan of campaign of which he has no notion, under tactics of which he does not see the use."[4] Those words endeared him to Theodore Roosevelt, who would one day appoint Holmes to the Supreme Court.

After the war, Holmes attended Harvard Law School and practiced law in Boston. He brought his philosophical training to bear on the law and soon made his mark as a legal scholar by publishing a treatise called *The Common Law*. The common law is law developed by judges through court decisions, as opposed to law set forth by legislative statutes. Holmes's book aspired to unify the different branches of the common law based on scientific principles. Though perhaps not wholly successful in that endeavor, Holmes helped pioneer an idea that was to revolutionize scholarly thinking about the law. He said, in essence, that law was not *found*, but rather *made*. Law, in other words, is what judges and courts do in exercising their power, and it is thus a product of historical, social, and political context. And since law is made, not found, Holmes urged conscious reform of the law to put it on a rational and scientific footing.

Holmes was nominated to the Supreme Judicial Court of Massachusetts in 1882, where he served—first as Associate Justice and then as Chief Justice—for twenty years. He relished the work, which brought together the real-life grit of family law, property disputes, and criminal prosecutions with the great theoretical questions posed by the law. In 1902, President Theodore Roosevelt nominated him for the Supreme Court, where he was to sit as an Associate Justice for the next twenty-nine years.

Perhaps Holmes's greatest contribution to the Court's jurisprudence was his insistence on judicial deference to the political branches in matters of economic regulation. Like those of Justice Fields before him, Holmes's most famous opinions were written in dissent—though, ironically, Holmes fought *against* precisely the ideas that Justice Field had advocated. In its infamous 1905 decision in *Lochner v. New York,* the Supreme Court struck down a New York law that limited bakery workers' hours to sixty per week, or ten hours per day. Echoing former Justice Field, the Court held this was an unconstitutional interference in the bakeries' liberty to contract with their workers. Holmes issued a vigorous dissent, arguing that the Constitution did not enact any particular economic theory and that it was not the Court's role to impose its policy preferences on the elected branches of government.

This position, reiterated in several of Holmes's other dissents, is sometimes taken as a mark of Holmes's support for economic and social regulation. But in fact, Holmes was a realist who believed that the struggle between capital and labor must be re-

Associate Justice Oliver Wendell Holmes Jr., circa 1902.

solved politically or by interaction between the two. He was an elitist and no great friend of labor, but he did not think the courts should tip the scales one way or the other. And Holmes's belief in judicial restraint found expression in cases with notoriously nonprogressive results as well. In *Giles v. Harris,* Holmes wrote that the Court would not strike down state election laws that disfranchised African Americans because, in the end, it lacked any power to restrict state action in this sphere. And Holmes famously upheld the states' constitutional authority to compel the sterilization of mentally retarded persons, stating bluntly that "[t]hree generations of imbeciles are enough."[5]

Holmes was one of the fastest and most eloquent writers in the history of the Supreme Court. For cases that were assigned Saturday, he had the opinion written by Monday or Tuesday and circulated by Wednesday. He prized brevity, which he thought conveyed ideas more powerfully: "The little snakes are the poisonous ones," he once wrote to a friend.[6] It has often been said that Holmes's opinions are easy to read and difficult to understand. Though his reasoning was sometimes cryptic, Holmes's brilliant prose made his opinions immortal.

In upholding restrictions on speech discouraging workers from registering for the draft during World War I, Holmes wrote that "the character of every act depends upon the circumstances in which it is done. . . . The most stringent protection of free speech would not protect a man in falsely shouting fire in a crowded theater and causing a panic."[7] Yet two years later, Holmes offered up one of the most compelling defenses of free speech ever penned:

> [W]hen men have realized that time has upset many fighting faiths, they may come to believe even more than they believe the very foundations of their own conduct that the ultimate good desired is better reached by free trade in ideas—that the best test of truth is the power of the thought to get itself accepted in the competition of the market, and that truth is the only ground upon which their wishes can safely be carried out. That, at any rate, is the theory of our Constitution.[8]

Holmes wanted to be, and ultimately was recognized as, the greatest legal thinker of his era. He had a remarkable personal intensity and a contagious passion for life, which did not wane with advancing years. The famous journalist Walter Lippmann described him as "a sage with the bearing of a cavalier; his presence is an incitement to high risks. . . . He wears wisdom like a gorgeous plume, and likes to tickle the sanctities between the ribs."[9] And author Henry James, a longtime friend, wrote of the sixty-two-year-old Holmes, "I have never seen anyone so unmodified through the years, who had equally *lived*. . . . Wendell has moved and moved like a full glass carried without spilling a drop."[10]

At eighty, Holmes wrote of his future, " 'Does the road lead uphill all the way? Yes—to the very end.' And one must *still* take one's chances."[11] He persevered on the Court until 1932, when he retired at the age of ninety. He died two years later. Like Justice Field before him, many of the positions he advocated in dissent came to prevail shortly after his death. His call for judicial deference to economic regulation ultimately carried the day, after the Court changed course in 1937 in the face of President Franklin Roosevelt's court-packing plan. He is universally considered one of the greatest Justices of all time.

JUSTICE JAMES MCREYNOLDS, by contrast, is commonly regarded as one of the *worst* justices ever to sit on the Supreme Court. While McReynolds is famous for his virulent opposition to the New Deal, his abysmal reputation stems mostly from his astonishingly mean and bigoted character.

Born in 1862 in Kentucky and educated at Vanderbilt and the University of Virginia, McReynolds was a Southern gentleman of the old school. He was reared on his parents' fundamentalist values and was rigid in his social and political views. "You can't paint a white rose red," he said of himself.[12] He had a strong sense of personal honor and moral righteousness, and he appeared to consider those who disagreed with him to be either stupid or evil. That view of the world led to much conflict in McReynolds's years as a Justice. As a friend of Justice McReynolds once said, "Men like . . . McReynolds are both stimulating and difficult: stimulating because we all need to be reminded of the importance of moral standards; and difficult because at any moment they may convert an argument into a fight."[13]

McReynolds practiced law in Nashville, Tennessee, for twenty years before going to Washington, D.C., in 1903 to become an assistant attorney general in the administration of President Theodore Roosevelt. McReynolds achieved great success in Theodore Roosevelt administration's "trust-busting" campaign, and by the time he left government for private practice in 1912, he was widely—though inaccurately—considered a "liberal" and a "radical." His reputation as a vigorous government antitrust lawyer gained him the attention of Woodrow Wilson, and he was appointed Wilson's Attorney General in 1913. But McReynolds's acerbic character quickly made enemies in Congress and the administration. Wilson nominated McReynolds to the Supreme Court the following year, which some said was merely a ploy to get him out of the cabinet.

Although Justice McReynolds sat on the Court for twenty-six years, his character made him ill-suited to the job. He had difficulty submitting to debate among equals and to the necessary restrictions on his freedom to advocate his views publicly. Referred to as "the rudest man in Washington," he was abrasive both on and off the Court. He wrote comments such as "This makes me sick" on his colleagues' circulating opinions—hardly a recipe for collegiality. He was a self-professed anti-Semite and behaved badly toward Justices Brandeis and Cardozo, who were Jewish. For instance, he once ostentatiously read a newspaper during Cardozo's swearing-in ceremony. McReynolds was a lifetime bachelor who was apparently quite gallant in courting the ladies in Washington society. Though he put women on a social pedestal, he thought the notion of their participation in politics ridiculous. McReynolds was an unabashed racist and treated his black employees with a condescending paternalism. He infamously used his black valet, Harry Parker, as a human bird dog, requiring him to wade through icy water to fetch the ducks McReynolds shot when hunting.

McReynolds's work product on the Court was undistinguished. He wrote short opinions composed mostly of quotations from lower-court opinions, citing little or no authority in support of the Court's decision and providing no discussion of the authority cited. Nevertheless, McReynolds gained national recognition as a strong friend of business with a deep antipathy to economic regulation. With the election of President Franklin Roosevelt in 1932, McReynolds became the leader of the famed "Four Horsemen of the Apocalypse"—the four Justices who repeatedly voted to strike down New Deal legislation on various constitutional grounds. McReynolds thought the New Deal heralded the destruction of the "American system," and he saw the Court as the last bastion protecting the country against socialism. Moreover, he personally disliked Franklin Roosevelt, whom he described as "that crippled jackass" in the White House. Roosevelt returned the sentiment, and at his famous weekly poker games the wild card was referred to as Justice McReynolds.

The story of how President Roosevelt, in 1937, sought to overcome the Supreme Court's opposition to New Deal legislation by "packing" the Court has been mentioned. What is less well known is that the court-packing plan was in fact derived from a similar plan proposed by McReynolds himself in 1914, when he was Attorney General. McReynolds had excluded the Supreme Court from his plan, but suggested that a new judge should be appointed for each lower federal court judge who turned seventy while on the bench, in order to ensure efficiency in the lower courts. President Roosevelt took ironic pleasure in adapting

McReynolds's idea to the task of defeating McReynolds and his fellow conservatives on the Court.

The President's plan to pack the Court with sympathetic justices did not succeed. It is often said that the court-packing plan helped precipitate the famed "switch in time that saved nine." The phrase—a play on the saying "a stitch in time saves nine"—refers to a perceived shift in position by Justice Owen Roberts. Many perceived that Justice Roberts, after voting to invalidate New Deal legislation in several cases, suddenly reversed course in a 1937 case, *West Coast Hotel Co. v. Parrish,* in order to protect the Court from the President's court-packing plan.[14] Later accounts, however, have indicated that Justice Roberts cast his vote before President Roosevelt even announced his plan.[15] In any event, 1937 marked the demise of the Four Horsemen and the beginning of the end for Justice McReynolds. McReynolds retired in 1941, three days before his seventy-ninth birthday. He had dissented more often than any other Justice in the history of the Supreme Court. When he died in 1946, not a single one of his fellow Justices attended his funeral.

IF ONE TRIED TO imagine the antithesis of Justice McReynolds, Justice William O. Douglas might come close to the mark. Whereas McReynolds was passionately conservative and lived by a rigid moral code, Douglas was one of the most liberal Justices ever to sit on the Supreme Court, and his libertine conduct helped earn him the moniker "Wild Bill."

Douglas was born in Minnesota in 1898. His father died when he was five years old, and his mother raised him and his siblings on her own in the town of North Yakima, Washington. Douglas's mother called him her "treasure" and told him that he would someday be President of the United States. It was an ambition he tried to fulfill for much of his life. After attending college in Washington state, Douglas was admitted to Columbia Law

School. He financed his trip to New York by shepherding a couple of thousand sheep on freight trains headed east from Washington.

He married his hometown sweetheart while in law school, and she worked as a teacher to help put him through school. Douglas visited his wife on weekends but kept her existence a secret from his classmates. He excelled in law school, and soon after graduating, he rose to become one of the leading law professors in the country. His scholarship on business law reform gained the attention of officials in President Franklin Roosevelt's administration, and by 1937, Douglas was appointed chairman of the Securities and Exchange Commission. He gained national attention as an aggressive reformer who brought about a dramatic reorganization of the New York Stock Exchange. President Roosevelt nominated Douglas to the Supreme Court in 1939. At the age of forty, he was one of the youngest Justices in Supreme Court history.

Douglas's ambitions went beyond the Court, however. He had his eye on the White House, and nearly got there. He was President Roosevelt's first choice for a running mate in 1944, but backroom politicking deprived him of the nomination. Truman invited him to be his running mate in 1948, but Douglas declined, thinking Truman would lose. At the end of the day his efforts came to naught, and he remained a Justice for thirty-five years.

On the Court, Douglas became one of most liberal Justices in American history, most often arguing his cause in dissent. Douglas was a First Amendment absolutist, fighting for virtually unhindered freedom of speech even as the Communist scare rocked the country. In 1965 he wrote the opinion for the Court in *Griswold v. Connecticut,* which held that the Constitution forbade government from prohibiting the sale of contraceptives, and thus laid the foundation for *Roe v. Wade.* He was a strong opponent of the Vietnam War, which he believed was unconstitutional. In his capacity as circuit justice for the Ninth Circuit, he sought unsuccessfully to stop draftees from being sent to Vietnam and to block the bombing of Cambodia in 1972.

Despite his meteoric rise in Washington politics, and the high office in which he came to rest, Douglas retained his Western roots. He wore a Stetson, spoke with a Western accent, struck his matches on his shoe or his pants seat, and maintained an ostentatious irreverence for the social traditions of the capital. He was a legendary storyteller, and according to President Roosevelt at least, a pretty good poker player. Most notably, he loved the outdoors, especially the mountains, and was widely traveled. Every summer he returned to Washington state, where he stayed in his log cabin and hiked and camped in the Cascade Mountains.

There is a story about how, during the summer of 1970, some lawyers sought to bring an emergency application in a case to Justice Douglas while he was camping in the Cascades. The lawyers, wearing their business suits and bearing briefcases, hiked out to find Douglas on a remote trail. They represented protesters who had been arrested in the course of a peaceful demonstration against the Vietnam War. Given Douglas's record, the attorneys were sure that he would grant their clients emergency relief. But what they didn't realize was that one of the few things Douglas hated more than Richard Nixon and the Vietnam War was being interrupted during a camping trip. It was close to twilight when the lawyers found Douglas, but he told them to come back in the morning when he would issue his ruling. They reluctantly tramped back toward the trailhead. When they returned the next morning, they found a handwritten note on a scrap of paper under a rock. It read, "Denied—William O. Douglas."

Douglas's love of the outdoors made him an avid conservationist, and he worked to preserve wild and open space around the country. When *The Washington Post* wrote favorably of plans to construct a road along the towpath of the Chesapeake & Ohio Canal near Washington, D.C., Douglas challenged the paper's

Associate Justice William O. Douglas on the Potomac River.

editors to hike the 185-mile towpath with him. Several accepted and the publicity sparked by the hike helped lead to the preservation of the old towpath as a national historical park. Douglas spearheaded many similar events intended to gain support for the protection of natural places around the country.

Despite his achievements in some spheres, Douglas's personal life was more troubled. In 1951, he became the first Supreme Court Justice ever to be divorced when he left his wife of twenty-eight years for another woman. In 1963, at the age of sixty-five, he divorced his second wife and married a twenty-three-year-old. Three years later, he divorced his third wife and married a twenty-two-year-old. Each successive divorce imposed further financial burdens on Douglas, and by his late sixties, he was nearly destitute. Meanwhile, in the face of opposition from President Nixon and conservatives in Congress, Douglas became increasingly paranoid during his latter years that he was being subjected to government surveillance.

The disorder in Douglas's personal life perhaps carried over into his work on the Court. Justice Brennan once said that Douglas's last decade on the Court was characterized by "slovenliness" and errors. Douglas at last stepped down from the Court in 1974 after suffering a severe stroke. He had served thirty-five years on the bench. In the course of his tenure, he had faced formal impeachment charges in the House on at least two occasions for his actions on and off the bench. He had written more than one thousand full opinions, including nearly five hundred dissents. Nearly half of the latter were solo dissents, earning him the nickname "the Lone Ranger." He wrote thirty-two books, including a bestselling autobiography and numerous accounts of his travels around the world. Douglas died in 1980. He was buried in Arlington National Cemetery with a tombstone inscribed, as Douglas had requested, WILLIAM O. DOUGLAS, PRIVATE, UNITED STATES ARMY.

BRITISH ACTOR DONALD SINDEN once said, "Actors ought to be larger than life. You come across quite enough ordinary, nondescript people in daily life and I don't see why you should be subjected to them on the stage too." If the Supreme Court bench can be likened to a stage, these four men were larger-than-life actors who certainly made "the play" interesting. Each was molded by the place from which he came: Field by the California frontier, Holmes by patrician Boston, McReynolds by the Old South, and

Douglas by the mountains of Washington state. Each was shaped by and shaped the times in which he lived: Field by the opening of the far West; Holmes by the Civil War, the industrial revolution, and the First World War; McReynolds by the passing of the old economic order and the advent of the New Deal; and Douglas by the transition from the New Deal to the Red scares and later to the Vietnam War. They held radically different ideas about the proper relationship between government and business, between security and free speech, and each held his ideas passionately. Each made his mark on the Court's jurisprudence, not usually by writing for the majority, but in dissent. None hesitated to go it alone when his principles so required. Not all of these men were likable, and indeed the beliefs and conduct of a couple of them were at times unworthy of the great office they held.

Their stories may tell us something of what sort of character we should look for in a Justice of the Supreme Court. But whatever lessons we may draw from them, these larger-than-life personalities will always be remembered.

GONE BUT NOT FORGOTTEN

Judicial Retirement

———— // ————

Much attention has been focused on how Justices join the Court and what they have done in their careers in advance of their nominations. Justices' departures from the Court have received less attention. Justices are, to a fault, dedicated to their judicial role, the Court itself, and their service to the country. The decision to leave the Court is never an easy one, and a Justice's reasons are deeply personal. This chapter discusses the laws governing departures, reasons Justices have left the Court, and Justices' post-Court activities.

THE LAWS GOVERNING JUSTICES' pensions have changed greatly over the years. The first statute on judicial pensions was passed in 1869. It provided that Justices who reached the age of seventy and had at least ten years of service could resign their seat; they were entitled to receive for life the same salary to which they were entitled at the time of their resignation.[1] Resignation terminated the Justice's judicial office. He (and they were all male until

1981!) could no longer participate in the work of the Supreme Court or any other federal court.

That changed in 1937. At that time, the Supreme Court had struck down a number of the Roosevelt administration's New Deal statutes. In order to ensure that the rest of the New Deal would be upheld, President Franklin D. Roosevelt proposed the plan under which one Justice would be added to the Supreme Court for one over the age of seventy. Some in Congress supported a mandatory retirement age for Justices, but President Roosevelt would not compromise.[2]

Congress instead passed the Retirement (Sumners-McCarran) Act of March 1, 1937. The act gave Supreme Court Justices the option to take "senior status," an option that federal circuit and district court judges had had since 1919.[3] The 1937 law provided that Justices who reached the age of seventy and had at least ten years of service as a federal judge could *retire* to senior status, rather than resign as a federal judge.[4] Under this provision, retired Justices remained federal judges. They could not participate in the work of the Supreme Court but could still perform judicial duties in any other federal court, whether district or circuit. The act also allowed Justices to continue to receive their salary.[5] The first Justice to avail himself of the senior status option was Justice Willis Van Devanter, a conservative who had opposed the Roosevelt administration's New Deal programs and had become known as one of the Four Horsemen.[6]

In the 1980s, the law changed again. Justices now may take senior status by satisfying the "Rule of Eighty."[7] This rule refers to the fact that Justices who reach the age of sixty-five may retire if the sum of their age and years of judicial service is at least eighty. They continue to draw for life a salary equal to that in place when they retired.[8] In addition, Justices who retire to senior status may continue to receive the "salary of the office"— which means they are entitled to any pay raise afforded to active

Justices—by performing judicial duties or other government service equal to three months of work by an active Justice.[9]

Although judges on lower courts who take senior status are entitled to continue to sit on cases in their home court or elsewhere if so designated, Supreme Court Justices are permitted to sit anywhere *but* the Court to which they were confirmed. This principle was firmly established within the Court due to events arising out of the retirement of Justice William O. Douglas. Justice Douglas's health had been failing for some time and severely deteriorated after he suffered a stroke at the end of 1974.[10] During the first sittings of the 1975 Term, Douglas was too ill to remain on the bench for oral argument, and his colleagues took the extraordinary step of refusing to assign him any opinions to write.[11]

On November 12, 1975, Justice Douglas submitted his retirement.[12] After Justice John Paul Stevens took his place, however, Justice Douglas expressed his view that he should remain able to participate in all cases on which certiorari had been granted prior to his retirement.[13] Justice Douglas went so far as to announce that he planned to write an opinion in *Buckley v. Valeo,* an important campaign finance case.[14] He then wrote an opinion and attempted to have it circulated to the active Justices.[15] At that point, the active Justices intervened. Chief Justice Burger wrote a memo, signed by all of the Justices, explaining that as a retired Justice, Justice Douglas was no longer entitled to participate in oral argument or the Court's Conference or to vote and issue opinions in cases.[16]

THERE ARE THREE BROAD categories of reasons for which most Justices have left the Court. The first is death in office. Fifty Supreme Court Justices have died during their service as active Justices.[17] The retirement provisions described above have helped to decrease the incidence of Justices remaining in office while infirm because Justices do not need to do so to retain their salary. Since the 1937 Retirement Act, only eight Justices have died in office, and Chief Justice William H. Rehnquist is the only Justice who has died in office since 1954.[18] The vast majority of Justices since that time have taken senior status.[19]

The second type of reason frequently cited by Justices who have resigned or retired is advanced age or ill health.[20] Because Justices hold their offices during "good behavior," which typically amounts to a life appointment, Justices are often quite advanced in years at the time they retire. Of course, the physical burdens of the office now are substantially less than they were in the early years of the Court when the Justices rode circuit. Justice John Blair Jr., who resigned in 1796, and Justice Benjamin R. Curtis, who resigned in 1857, cited the circuit-riding responsibilities as among their reasons for resigning.[21]

On at least two occasions, members of the Court have urged their colleagues to step down when deteriorating health was interfering with their ability to serve effectively. As described above, Justice Douglas's colleagues pressed him to retire after his 1974 stroke left him unable to walk, in constant pain, and increasingly mentally disoriented. As Douglas began casting votes that contradicted his prior positions and suffering bouts of pain that forced him to leave oral arguments, the other Justices effectively stripped him of his judicial functions in a remarkable effort to encourage him to step down.[22] A majority of the Court had similarly banded together and agreed to suggest retirement to Justice Oliver Wendell Holmes Jr. in 1932. Justice Holmes was noticeably fatigued and, at nearly ninety-one years old, was the oldest justice to serve in history—a record that has yet to be surpassed to this day.[23] Chief Justice Charles Evan Hughes visited the Holmes residence one Sunday to carry out what he later called the "highly distasteful duty" of urging Justice Holmes to "not strain himself by continuing to carry the load when his strength was no longer equal to it."[24] Justice Holmes tendered his resignation to President Hoover the following day, writing that "[t]he condition of my health makes it a duty to break off connections that I cannot leave without deep regret."[25]

The third major reason Justices have given for resigning from the Court is to assume some other government office. This was the case for two early Justices who resigned to serve in *state* governments. Justice John Rutledge resigned in 1791 to become the Chief Justice of South Carolina.[26] John Jay, the first Chief Justice, resigned from the Court in 1795 to become governor of New York.[27]

Justice John Archibald Campbell resigned to join the Confederacy in 1861, shortly after the outbreak of the Civil War.[28] He served in the Confederacy as assistant secretary for war and was imprisoned by the Union army for several months after the war.[29] After his release, he returned to the practice of law and argued several cases before the Supreme Court, including the *Slaughter-House Cases.*[30]

Other Justices have resigned to serve the U.S. government. In 1877, Justice David Davis resigned to become a U.S. senator.[31] Justice Charles Evans Hughes resigned in 1916 to run for president on the Republican ticket; he lost the election, but was later reappointed and confirmed to the Court as Chief Justice in 1930.[32]

Other Justices took on executive branch roles. Justice James F. Byrnes resigned in 1942 to become the director of the Office of Economic Stabilization.[33] He became secretary of state under President Truman and was later governor of South Carolina.[34] Justice Arthur Goldberg resigned in 1965 to become the U.S. ambassador to the United Nations.[35]

Other Justices have resigned for personal reasons. For example, Justice Noah Swayne resigned in 1881 after extracting a promise from President Rutherford B. Hayes that he would appoint his friend Stanley Matthews to the Supreme Court seat

Swayne was vacating. President Hayes followed through, as promised.[36] Justice Tom C. Clark retired in 1967 to avoid possible conflicts of interest that might arise after his son, Ramsey Clark, was appointed U.S. Attorney General.[37] I retired in 2006 in part to spend more time with my husband, John, who was in poor health.

Not all of the personal reasons have been positive, however. As mentioned earlier, Justice Abe Fortas resigned in 1969 due to an ethics scandal.[38] *Life* magazine published an article detailing financial ties between Justice Fortas and a financier who was indicted for fraud.[39] Prior to the indictment but while a member of the Court, Justice Fortas agreed to serve as a consultant for a foundation started by the financier, and he received money in compensation.[40] After the indictment, Justice Fortas returned the money, but a later Justice Department investigation revealed that the financier had agreed to pay Justice Fortas twenty thousand dollars per year for life and then the same amount annually to Justice Fortas's wife.[41] The results of the investigation were shared with the members of the Court, and Justice Fortas resigned on May 14, 1969.[42]

MANY JUSTICES HAVE UNDERTAKEN significant nonjudicial and judicial activities after their retirement from the Court.

On the nonjudicial side, some Justices have taken full-time jobs, and others have devoted themselves to particular causes. For example, Justice John H. Clarke resigned in 1922 to campaign "for U.S. participation in the League of Nations and other peace efforts."[43] Justice Owen Roberts resigned in 1945 and became the dean of the University of Pennsylvania Law School.[44]

More recently, I have taken up the cause of promoting civics education in our nation's schools. I have focused particularly on creating and promoting a website—www.icivics.org—that provides games and teaching plans for use in educating middle school students about the three branches of government. Justice Stevens has also been active since his retirement in June 2010. He has given a number of speeches and published a book in 2011, *Five Chiefs,* about his experiences serving alongside five Chief Justices of the Court.

Other Justices, myself included, have undertaken other types of periodic government service, including, for example, speaking to foreign judges who visit the United States or traveling abroad to meet with lawyers and judges as the request of the U.S. Department of State.

A number of Justices have undertaken additional judicial service by sitting on the U.S. Courts of Appeals and even presiding over trials in federal district court. Since the advent of the senior status provision in 1937, eleven retired Justices have sat by designation.[45] Justices Willis Van Devanter—the first Justice to take senior status after the enactment of the 1937 act—and Justice Tom Clark both presided over trials in federal district court.[46] Justice Clark presided over the trial of one case that went to the Supreme Court. The case, *GTE Sylvania, Inc. v. Continental T.V., Inc.,*[47] involved antitrust law. The Supreme Court had considered and decided a legal question similar to that raised by the *GTE Sylvania* case in an earlier decision—one from which Justice Clark dissented.[48] When he instructed the jury in the *GTE Sylvania* case, however, Justice Clark explained the law in a manner consistent with his prior dissenting views.[49] The Ninth Circuit, sitting en banc—that is, the entire bench of judges, not just a three-judge panel—reversed him on appeal. Nevertheless, Justice Clark won out in the end when the Supreme Court granted certiorari on the case, overruled an earlier precedent, and ultimately vindicated Justice Clark's view of the law.[50]

Sitting on the lower federal courts after retirement can be particularly interesting for Justices who were not federal judges prior to their service on the Supreme Court. For example, Justice Stanley Reed had been the Solicitor General prior to his appointment to the Supreme Court,[51] but in retirement he sat regularly on the U.S. Court of Appeals for the District of Columbia Circuit, just down Capitol Hill from the Supreme Court.[52] Similarly, Justice Harold H. Burton, who had been a senator prior to his appointment to the Court, sat on the D.C. Circuit from 1959 to 1962.[53]

With my background in Arizona state government, I have found it particularly interesting to sit on the Courts of Appeals across the country. Participating in the operation of the various circuit courts has given me a better perspective on the work—and workload—of federal judges around the country. Each court has its own customs and ways of operating. And I have had the opportunity to meet so many interesting people from all walks of life along the way.

Many of the Court's more recently retired Justices have followed the practice of sitting by designation. Justice Potter Stewart, who was my predecessor on the Court, sat in several circuits after his retirement.[54] Justice Lewis Powell, a native of Richmond, Virginia, routinely sat with the Fourth Circuit Court of Appeals, which hears cases there. Justice Byron White sat on a variety of circuit courts in the 1990s.[55]

As of this writing, two of the three retired Justices currently sit on the circuit courts. Justice Souter sits often with the U.S. Court of Appeals for the First Circuit, in Boston, close to his native New Hampshire. I try to participate in sittings around three times a year. Thus far, I have sat on eleven of the thirteen Courts of Appeals around the country, with the only exceptions being the D.C. Circuit and the Federal Circuit, both of which are a bit more specialized than the numbered regional circuits.

A JUSTICE'S DECISION TO leave the Court is often very difficult. The senior status provisions have made the decision somewhat easier by providing Justices with an obvious way to continue serving the courts and the government more broadly by sitting by designation. Justice Lewis Powell summed up the feeling of many retired Justices, including me, when he said, "[T]he longest day is the day I don't have anything to do."[56] I have been blessed to stay busy with other important pursuits in the years since my retirement. And as I wrote to President George W. Bush in my letter relaying my decision to retire, I left the Court only with the utmost "respect for the integrity of the Court and its role under our Constitutional structure."[57]

SUPREME COURT "FIRSTS"

———————//———————

ONE OF THE THINGS I AM ASKED ABOUT MOST FREQUENTLY when I give public lectures is how it was to be the First Woman on the Supreme Court—or the FWOTSC, as I like to call myself. Acronyms are very important in Washington, D.C. Everyone who is important has one. And I tell people that it was great to be the first to do something, but I didn't want to be the last.

I also believe that it is challenging to be a "first." The first woman on the Court was carefully scrutinized by the press, the government, the lawyers, and the public. It is not always comfortable to be the object of so much attention. But the appointment of a woman to the Court opened countless doors to women all across the country. For that I am grateful. Nowadays, it is a thrill to look up at the bench during oral argument and see three women asking the inquisitive questions: Justices Ruth Bader Ginsburg, Sonia Sotomayor, and Elena Kagan.

Being so often referred to as a Supreme Court First naturally made me wonder about my predecessors. Although I was the first woman on the Supreme Court, there were many other firsts be-

The four women Justices: Sandra Day O'Connor, Sonia Sotomayor,
Ruth Bader Ginsburg, and Elena Kagan, circa 2010.

fore me. So I decided to compile a list of important "Firsts" on
the Supreme Court, and to try to learn a bit about what their
experiences could tell us about the institution and its evolution
over the years.

THE "FIRST" OF THE Firsts was, of course, John Jay, who was the
first Chief Justice of the United States. Jay was born in New York
in 1745 into a wealthy family.[1] He attended King's College (now
Columbia University) at the tender age of fourteen,[2] and decided
to study law. He became a successful young lawyer, and later a
prominent Whig leader. Jay also became an ardent advocate of

American independence, and was at the center of the political action during the Revolutionary War. He was one of the youngest members of the First Continental Congress (at age twenty-eight), and held very important diplomatic positions during the war, including Minister to Spain.

In 1784, Jay was named the first Secretary of Foreign Affairs, an office that later became Secretary of State. Although the Federalist Papers—a series of essays promoting the ratification of the Constitution—were published anonymously, it is known that Alexander Hamilton, James Madison, and John Jay were the authors. So valuable was Jay's service to the new federal government that when George Washington was elected President, he reportedly told Jay he could have his pick of positions.[3]

You know where this is leading, of course. Jay chose the position of Chief Justice of the United States, and the Senate confirmed him on September 24, 1789.[4] Scholars say that he chose the position because the Court was, at the time, a political experiment. And the Court was essential to the success of the new government, because it had an important role to play in making the system of federalism work.[5] It was crucial that it be led by someone with stature, someone who could lend legitimacy and prestige to the institution. Jay did exactly that. And to this day he is remembered more for his judicial statesmanship than for his judicial opinions.

There was not much business for the Court in the early years, and Jay was appointed by the President as a special envoy to Great Britain. He was sent to try to clear up lingering problems with the British that were threatening to erupt into another war.[6] Americans wanted compensation for goods and slaves seized by the British during the Revolutionary War and were angered by the continued British occupation of American frontier posts. The British had also created havoc for American shipping interests, preventing them from trading with certain British territories and seizing more than 250 U.S. ships in the Caribbean.[7]

In time, Jay successfully negotiated what came to be called the Jay Treaty. He then returned to the United States, where, as mentioned, he learned that in his absence his friends had nominated him for governor of New York. What's more, he was elected[8]—without any campaigning or fund-raising on his part.

As a result, in 1795, Jay became the first Chief Justice to resign. He thought the Supreme Court would never amount to much. When he stepped down, President Washington nominated John Rutledge of South Carolina to the position—setting in motion the first confirmation battle over a Supreme Court Justice.[9] The trouble began four days after Rutledge was nominated, when Rutledge deeply angered the Federalists—who controlled the Senate—with public criticism of the Jay Treaty. The treaty was quite unpopular at the time, because Jay had secured very little of what most Americans wanted and had given up a great deal, including commercial access to the British West Indies. In truth, most historians think that this was the best that the United States could do at the time, because the country had little bargaining power. The Senate thought the same thing and ratified the treaty despite popular uproar against it.

Rutledge called the treaty a "prostitution of the dearest rights of free men,"[10] even saying that he would rather George Washington die than he sign the Jay Treaty.[11] This was probably another first—the first time that a nominee to the Supreme Court publicly wished for the death of the man who nominated him! One expects that it was also a Supreme Court "last." Rutledge was attacked viciously for his speech and accused of being mentally unsound. And although he had already become a Justice through a recess appointment, when the nomination was put to the Senate (as it had to be, once they were back in session), Rutledge was rejected by that body in a close vote.[12]

This first nomination battle presented the first conflict over the meaning of that part of the appointments clause of the Constitution, which says that Presidents shall appoint federal judges and Justices of the Supreme Court "by and with the Advice and Consent of the Senate." The important legal question, of course, is what exactly "advice and consent" means, and how much of an active role the Senate should play in reviewing the qualifications or politics of judicial nominees. The fight over Rutledge's nomination is an important example in part because many senators at the time had been involved in the drafting of the Constitution.[13]

After Rutledge's statements on the Jay Treaty, he was attacked as incompetent and insane. But his speech was the only real evidence of insanity that anyone cited. Some sources suggest that Rutledge was quite depressed at the time because of the recent loss of his wife.[14] But private letters and accounts of the Senate deliberations at the time make it clear that, at least as far as the senators were concerned, it was the Jay Treaty that was on their minds, even if Rutledge's sanity was on their lips.[15]

It is clear that these early senators understood the Senate's advice and consent power to be very robust. They thought that it permitted them to reject a candidate not only because he was objectively unqualified, but also because they found his political views extreme.[16] It seems that this view still prevails today.

So whatever happened to poor Mr. Rutledge? Well, if he was not mentally unwell before the confirmation process, he apparently was afterward. Thirteen days after the Senate rejected his nomination, he tried to drown himself.[17] He did not succeed, thanks to some passing Good Samaritans who rescued him. They got no thanks from Rutledge, who reportedly protested that "he had long been a Judge and knew no Law that forbid a man to take away his own life."[18]

A HUNDRED YEARS OR so later, there was another set of firsts in store for the Court. Each Justice hires four law clerks (although the Chief Justice is allowed to hire five). They are typically recent law graduates with distinguished academic records. They work for their Justice for one year, conducting research, writing memos, and sometimes assisting with the drafting of opinions.

But Justices did not always have law clerks around to help out with their work. The position of the clerk was unknown to the American judiciary until it was introduced by Justice Horace Gray. Gray was something of a prodigy—he graduated from Harvard College at seventeen, and while at Harvard Law School he helped develop the case method for studying law.[19] So it is perhaps no surprise that he was ahead of the curve in another respect, too. In 1882, he was the first Supreme Court Justice to hire a law clerk. Congress did not allocate any money for this position, so Justice Gray paid the clerk's salary out of his own pocket. He had done the same thing when he was Chief Justice of the Supreme Judicial Court of Massachusetts.[20]

A few years later, Congress began allocating money to pay the salary of one law clerk for each Justice.[21] But it took several decades for the system as we know it today to take root. Before that, Justices typically hired local attorneys and kept them on as long as they could. It was not until 1974 that a Justice first hired four law clerks, which today is the norm. For a Washington bureaucracy, this is a remarkably slow growth!

Although I was the first woman to sit on the Supreme Court, I like to remind myself that there were, in fact, women who blazed some of that trail before me. One was Lucile Lomen, who in 1944 became the first woman law clerk at the Supreme Court. She was a graduate of the University of Washington School of Law[22] and was hired by Justice Douglas after he found himself unable to secure a qualified male clerk. World War II had depleted the ranks of law schools, and the professors who recommended clerks sent word to the Justice that they couldn't find anyone they thought worthy of the position. Justice Douglas wrote back to one of them and asked whether they also meant that they had no qualified *women* for the position. It turned out that they did, but apparently it had not occurred to them to recommend one.

Douglas hired Lomen and later declared her to have "a fine mind and a firm foundation in the law."[23] Nonetheless, he did not hire another woman until nearly thirty years later, in 1972.[24] In fact, *none* of the Justices hired another woman until 1966.[25] The numbers have gone up slowly, but steadily, over the decades— from 0 percent in 1970, to 9 percent in 1980, to 24 percent in 1990, to 28 percent in 2000.[26] In 2011, there were thirty-nine law clerks, and thirteen of them were women. That was about 33 percent women—still underrepresentation, because women now make up more than 50 percent of incoming law school classes, but far better than it used to be.

In 1948, Justice Felix Frankfurter hired the first African American law clerk.[27] The clerk was William T. Coleman Jr., who went on to a distinguished career at the NAACP and served in the cabinet of President Gerald Ford. Coleman had graduated magna cum laude from Harvard Law School, but no law firm in his hometown of Philadelphia would hire him. He eventually landed a job as a law clerk on the Third Circuit, and then worked for Frankfurter, but remarkably, after all of that, he still could not get a job at a firm in Philadelphia.[28]

Justice Frankfurter was the first to break the color line for clerks, but ten years later, when Professor Albert Sacks of Harvard Law School urged him to hire Ruth Bader Ginsburg, he refused to break his tradition of hiring only male law clerks. This was despite the fact that Ruth had tied for first in her class at Columbia Law School. She later became the first tenured woman professor at her alma mater, and, of course, was the second woman appointed to the Supreme Court.

Another clerk-related first happened in 1962, when Justice Bryon White was appointed to the Supreme Court. It was the first time that a person who had previously served as a clerk on the Supreme Court became a Justice of that same court.[29] Of course, that has happened several times since then. Chief Justice Rehnquist clerked for Justice Robert Jackson. Justice Stevens clerked for Justice Wiley Rutledge. And Justice Stephen Breyer clerked for Justice Arthur Goldberg.[30] But perhaps the culmina-

Portrait of Belva Lockwood, circa 1880.

tion of this trend came with Chief Justice John Roberts. He was the first Supreme Court Justice to take the seat of a Justice for whom he had clerked, Chief Justice William Rehnquist.

NOT ALL OUR IMPORTANT firsts have been about Justices and law clerks. Belva Lockwood was a widow and a young mother who moved to Washington, D.C., at the end of the Civil War. She was also a lawyer, and her work supported her family. When she applied for admission to the bar of the Supreme Court in 1876, her application was denied with the following statement: "By the uniform practice of this court, from its organization to the present time, and by the fair construction of its rules, none but men are admitted to practice before it as attorneys and counselors. . . . The court does not feel called upon to make a change, until such a change is required by statute."[31]

Another person might have taken that denial as a rejection. Belva Lockwood chose to take it as advice. She lobbied Congress relentlessly to pass that statute, and she succeeded. Three years after the Supreme Court refused to allow women to practice in its hallowed halls, President Rutherford B. Hayes signed a bill into law that allowed women to practice before any federal court. On March 3, 1879, Belva Lockwood became the first woman admitted to practice before the Supreme Court.[32] Shortly thereafter, she made history a second time when she represented Caroline Kaiser in *Kaiser v. Stickney,* and became the first woman to argue before the Supreme Court.[33]

RELIGIOUS DIVERSITY WAS ALSO a long time coming to the Court. At first, all of the Justices were Protestants. The first Catholic was appointed to the Supreme Court in 1836—it was Chief Justice Roger Brooke Taney. Historians have found no evidence that Taney's Catholicism was a factor to President Andrew Jackson,

Associate Justice Louis D. Brandeis.

who nominated him. The most important thing to Jackson was that Taney was a loyal Jacksonian. And although there was some criticism in the media of Taney's Catholicism, those who were opposed to his nomination seem to have been more concerned about Taney's support for Jackson than his faith.[34] The second Catholic wasn't appointed until almost sixty years later, but since then there has always been at least one Catholic on the Supreme Court.[35] Indeed, today there are six, another first.

It was not until 1916 that the Court had its first Jewish Justice, Louis Brandeis. Anti-Semitism was a force in American politics at the time, but there are different accounts about how much that had to do with the very heated opposition to Brandeis's nomination. Brandeis was well known as the "People's Lawyer." He was a strong critic of big business, and a strong defender of Congress's constitutional power to pass socioeconomic legislation, which was a hotly contested issue at the time. Brandeis's confirmation hearings were long and heated—though Brandeis followed them from afar. He did not attend, because it did not become customary for a nominee to attend his own confirmation hearings until Felix Frankfurter did so twenty-three years later.[36]

A FEW YEARS AFTER Frankfurter left the Court, the Court received its first African American Justice—the remarkable Thurgood Marshall. Justice Marshall was an important figure long before he was on the Court, of course, because he helped litigate cases like *Brown v. Board of Education,* and bring an end to de jure segregation in this country. But he also had a tremendous influence on the Court because of the special perspective he brought with him. His was the eye of a lawyer who saw the deepest wounds in the social fabric, and who used the law to help heal them. And he brought the things he had seen, the world as he knew it, into our oral arguments and conference meetings. He knew as well as anyone that, as Justice Frankfurter once wrote, the Court "should not be ignorant as judge of what we know as men."[37]

I asked him once how he managed to avoid becoming despondent from the injustices he saw. Instead of responding directly, he told me about the time he and his mentor, Charles Hamilton Houston, the vice dean at Howard University School of Law, traveled to Loudoun County, Virginia, to help a man on trial for his life. George Crawford had been indicted by an all-white grand jury of murdering a white woman from a well-to-do Virginia family, as well as her white maid. Despite their defense challenge to the exclusion of African Americans from the jury, Crawford was convicted of murder by an all-white jury and sentenced to life. "You know something is wrong with the government's case," Justice Marshall told me, "when a Negro only gets life for murdering a white woman."

After the trial, Justice Marshall said, the media asked if Crawford planned an appeal based on the exclusion of African Americans from the jury. "Crawford asked, 'Mr. Houston, I got life this time and if I have another trial, could they kill me the next time?' Charlie Houston told him yes. So Crawford told Charlie: 'Tell them the defendant rests.'

"I still have mixed feelings about that case," Justice Marshall added. "I just don't believe that guy got a fair shake. But what are you going to do?" he asked. "There are only two choices in life: stop and go on. You tell me, what would you pick?" Thurgood taught us all that you go on, but that you cannot forget. You must learn from what you have seen and bring that knowledge to your practice of law and your practice as a judge. We will always be grateful for that example.

ANOTHER SUPREME COURT FIRST came in 1962, when Justice Byron White was nominated to the Supreme Court: He was the first Supreme Court Justice to ever lead the NFL in rushing in a rookie season. And I can safely predict that he will be the last. White, of course, was a marvelous athlete, and he is also responsible for another important first—he was the first Justice that we know to have played basketball on the Highest Court of the Land, which, as I mentioned earlier, is what we call the basketball court just above the courtroom in the Supreme Court building.

But White *was not* the first Supreme Court Justice to have been a professional athlete. That honor goes to the Justice who hired Byron White as a law clerk: Chief Justice Frederick Moore

Chief Justice Rehnquist and Justices O'Connor, Brennan, and White
at Independence Hall, Philadelphia.

Vinson. Fred Vinson was a good baseball player. He once said—
and he was apparently only half-joking—that the reason he did
not more actively seek to play in the major leagues was that he
could not get along with umpires.[38] Maybe he became a Chief

Justice by following that old saying "If you can't beat 'em, join 'em." In any case, Vinson *did* actually try out for the majors, although he kept it a secret for a long time—whether because he was a flop or because his mother hated the idea of him playing professional baseball, we will never know.[39]

Even though Vinson never made it to the big leagues, he did play semiprofessional ball—earning twenty-five dollars a game (fifty for double-headers!) while he was in college, playing for any little minor-league team that would hire him.[40] His baseball skills also turned out to be handy even after he became a lawyer. During the first few years of his practice, when business was slow, he would earn some money on the side as a freelance baseball player. Budding lawyers should keep this lesson from Chief Justice Vinson in mind: diversify, diversify, diversify.

WE CAN LEARN A LOT from Supreme Court Firsts. And I am honored to have had the opportunity to be one of them.

APPENDIX A

*The Declaration of Independence
of the United States of America*

———//———

This volume includes a copy of the Constitution of the United States because, ultimately, any collection of stories about the Supreme Court is a collection of stories about our Constitution. As our great Chief Justice John Marshall said: "We must never forget that it is a Constitution we are expounding." I carry a copy in my purse wherever I go. I am also including a copy of the Declaration of Independence because we need to remember that the story of our Constitution began with the brave decision of our Framers to reject government by a distant monarchy and to begin an experiment in securing life, liberty, and the pursuit of happiness through a constitutional democracy—a decision that continues to guide us today. The legacy of these documents is reflected in the experiences of the men and women who have served on the Supreme Court, but in the end, these texts remain the foundation for the stories of all of us who are Americans.

In CONGRESS, July 4, 1776

The unanimous Declaration of the thirteen united States of America

When in the Course of human events, it becomes necessary for one people to dissolve the political bands which have connected them with another, and to assume, among the Powers of the earth, the separate and equal station to which the Laws of Nature and of Nature's God entitle them, a decent respect to the opinions of mankind requires that they should declare the causes which impel them to the separation.

We hold these truths to be self-evident, that all men are created equal, that they are endowed by their Creator with certain unalienable Rights, that among these are Life, Liberty, and the pursuit of Happiness.—That to secure these rights, Governments are instituted among Men, deriving their just powers from the consent of the governed,—That whenever any Form of Government becomes destructive of these ends, it is the Right of the People to alter or to abolish it, and to institute new Government, laying its foundation on such principles and organizing its powers in such form, as to them shall seem most likely to effect their Safety and Happiness. Prudence, indeed, will dictate that Governments long established should not be changed for light and transient causes; and accordingly all experience hath shown, that mankind are more disposed to suffer, while evils are sufferable, than to right themselves by abolishing the forms to which they are accustomed. But when a long train of abuses and usurpations, pursuing invariably the same Object evinces a design to reduce them under absolute Despotism, it is their right, it is their duty, to throw off such Government, and to provide new Guards for their future security.—Such has been the patient sufferance of these Colonies; and such is now the necessity which constrains them to alter their former Systems of Government. The history of the present King of Great Britain is a history of repeated injuries and usurpations, all having in direct object the establishment of an absolute Tyranny over these States. To prove this, let Facts be submitted to a candid world.

He has refused his Assent to Laws, the most wholesome and necessary for the public good.

He has forbidden his Governors to pass Laws of immediate and pressing importance, unless suspended in their operation till his Assent should be obtained; and when so suspended, he has utterly neglected to attend to them.

He has refused to pass other Laws for the accommodation of large districts of people, unless those people would relinquish the right of Representation in the Legislature, a right inestimable to them and formidable to tyrants only.

He has called together legislative bodies at places unusual, uncomfortable, and distant from the depository of their Public Records, for the sole purpose of fatiguing them into compliance with his measures.

He has dissolved Representative Houses repeatedly, for opposing with manly firmness his invasions on the rights of the people.

He has refused for a long time, after such dissolutions, to cause others to be elected; whereby the Legislative Powers, incapable of Annihilation, have returned to the People at large for their exercise; the State remaining in the mean time exposed to all the dangers of invasion from without, and convulsions within.

He has endeavoured to prevent the population of these States; for that purpose obstructing the Laws of Naturalization of Foreigners; refusing to pass others to encourage their migration hither, and raising the conditions of new Appropriations of Lands.

He has obstructed the Administration of Justice, by refusing his Assent to Laws for establishing Judiciary Powers.

He has made judges dependent on his Will alone, for the tenure of their offices, and the amount and payment of their salaries.

He has erected a multitude of New Offices, and sent hither swarms of Officers to harass our People, and eat out their substance.

He has kept among us, in times of peace, Standing Armies without the Consent of our legislatures.

He has affected to render the Military independent of and superior to the Civil Power.

He has combined with others to subject us to a jurisdiction foreign to our constitution, and unacknowledged by our laws; giving his Assent to their Acts of pretended legislation: For quartering large bodies of armed troops among us: For protecting them, by a mock Trial, from Punishment for any Murders which they should commit on the Inhabitants of these States:

For cutting off our Trade with all parts of the world:

For imposing taxes on us without our Consent:

For depriving us, in many cases, of the benefits of Trial by Jury:

For transporting us beyond Seas to be tried for pretended offences:

For abolishing the free System of English Laws in a neighbouring Province, establishing therein an Arbitrary government, and enlarging its Boundaries so as to render it at once an example and fit instrument for introducing the same absolute rule into these Colonies:

For taking away our Charters, abolishing our most valuable Laws, and altering fundamentally the Forms of our Governments:

For suspending our own Legislatures, and declaring themselves invested with power to legislate for us in all cases whatsoever.

He has abdicated Government here, by declaring us out of his Protection and waging War against us.

He has plundered our seas, ravaged our Coasts, burnt our towns, and destroyed the lives of our people.

He is at this time transporting large armies of foreign Mercenaries to compleat the works of death, desolation and tyranny, already begun with circumstances of Cruelty & perfidy scarcely paralleled in the most barbarous ages, and totally unworthy of the Head of a civilized nation.

He has constrained our fellow Citizens taken Captive on the high Seas to bear Arms against their Country, to become the executioners of their friends and Brethren, or to fall themselves by their Hands.

He has excited domestic insurrections amongst us, and has endeavoured to bring on the inhabitants of our frontiers, the merciless Indian Savages, whose known rule of warfare, is an undistinguished destruction of all ages, sexes and conditions.

In every stage of these Oppressions We have Petitioned for Redress in the most humble terms: Our repeated Petitions have been answered only by repeated injury. A Prince, whose character is thus marked by every act which may define a Tyrant, is unfit to be the ruler of a free people.

Nor have We been wanting in attention to our Brittish brethren. We have warned them from time to time of attempts by their legislature to extend an unwarrantable jurisdiction over us. We have reminded them of the circumstances of our emigration and settlement here. We have appealed to their native justice and magnanimity, and we have conjured them by the ties of our common kindred to disavow these usurpations, which would inevitably interrupt our connections and correspondence. They too have been deaf to the voice of justice and of consanguinity. We must, therefore, acquiesce in the necessity, which denounces our Separation, and hold them, as we hold the rest of mankind, Enemies in War, in Peace Friends.

We, therefore, the Representatives of the United States of

America, in General Congress, Assembled, appealing to the Supreme Judge of the world for the rectitude of our intentions, do, in the Name, and by the Authority of the good People of these Colonies, solemnly publish and declare, That these United Colonies are, and of Right ought to be Free and Independent States; that they are Absolved from all Allegiance to the British Crown, and that all political connection between them and the State of Great Britain, is and ought to be totally dissolved; and that as Free and Independent States, they have full Power to levy War, conclude Peace, contract Alliances, establish Commerce, and to do all other Acts and Things which Independent States may of right do. And for the support of this Declaration, with a firm reliance on the Protection of Divine Providence, we mutually pledge to each other our Lives, our Fortunes and our sacred Honor.

Button Gwinnett	Benjamin Harrison	Lewis Morris
Lyman Hall	Thomas Nelson, Jr.	Richard Stockton
George Walton	Francis Lightfoot Lee	John Witherspoon
William Hooper	Carter Braxton	Francis Hopkinson
Joseph Hewes	Robert Morris	John Hart
John Penn	Benjamin Rush	Abraham Clark
Edward Rutledge	Benjamin Franklin	Josiah Bartlett
Thomas Heyward, Jr.	John Morton	William Whipple
Thomas Lynch, Jr.	George Clymer	Samuel Adams
Arthur Middleton	James Smith	John Adams
John Hancock	George Taylor	Robert Treat Paine
Samuel Chase	James Wilson	Elbridge Gerry
William Paca	George Ross	Stephen Hopkins
Thomas Stone	Caesar Rodney	William Ellery
Charles Carroll of Carrollton	George Read	Roger Sherman
George Wythe	Thomas McKean	Samuel Huntington
Richard Henry Lee	William Floyd	William Williams
Thomas Jefferson	Philip Livingston	Oliver Wolcott
	Francis Lewis	Matthew Thornton

APPENDIX B

The Constitution of the United States

———//———

We the People of the United States, in Order to form a more perfect Union, establish Justice, insure domestic Tranquility, provide for the common defence, promote the general Welfare, and secure the Blessings of Liberty to ourselves and our Posterity, do ordain and establish this Constitution for the United States of America.

ARTICLE. I.

Section. 1. All legislative Powers herein granted shall be vested in a Congress of the United States, which shall consist of a Senate and House of Representatives.

Section. 2. The House of Representatives shall be composed of Members chosen every second Year by the People of the several States, and the Electors in each State shall have the Qualifications requisite for Electors of the most numerous Branch of the State Legislature.

No Person shall be a Representative who shall not have attained to the Age of twenty five Years, and been seven Years a

Citizen of the United States, and who shall not, when elected, be an Inhabitant of that State in which he shall be chosen.

Representatives and direct Taxes shall be apportioned among the several States which may be included within this Union, according to their respective Numbers, which shall be determined by adding to the whole Number of free Persons, including those bound to Service for a Term of Years, and excluding Indians not taxed, three fifths of all other Persons. The actual Enumeration shall be made within three Years after the first Meeting of the Congress of the United States, and within every subsequent Term of ten Years, in such Manner as they shall by Law direct. The Number of Representatives shall not exceed one for every thirty Thousand, but each State shall have at Least one Representative; and until such enumeration shall be made, the State of New Hampshire shall be entitled to chuse three, Massachusetts eight, Rhode-Island and Providence Plantations one, Connecticut five, New-York six, New Jersey four, Pennsylvania eight, Delaware one, Maryland six, Virginia ten, North Carolina five, South Carolina five, and Georgia three.

When vacancies happen in the Representation from any State, the Executive Authority thereof shall issue Writs of Election to fill such Vacancies.

The House of Representatives shall chuse their Speaker and other Officers; and shall have the sole Power of Impeachment.

Section. 3. The Senate of the United States shall be composed of two Senators from each State, *chosen by the Legislature thereof,* for six Years; and each Senator shall have one Vote.

Immediately after they shall be assembled in Consequence of the first Election, they shall be divided as equally as may be into three Classes. The Seats of the Senators of the first Class shall be vacated at the Expiration of the second Year, of the second Class at the Expiration of the fourth Year, and of the third Class at the Expiration of the sixth Year, so that one third may be chosen every second Year; *and if Vacancies happen by Resignation, or otherwise, during the Recess of the Legislature of any State, the Executive thereof may make temporary Appointments until the next Meeting of the Legislature, which shall then fill such Vacancies.*

No Person shall be a Senator who shall not have attained to the Age of thirty Years, and been nine Years a Citizen of the United States, and who shall not, when elected, be an Inhabitant of that State for which he shall be chosen.

The Vice President of the United States shall be President of the Senate, but shall have no Vote, unless they be equally divided.

The Senate shall chuse their other Officers, and also a President pro tempore, in the Absence of the Vice President, or when he shall exercise the Office of President of the United States.

The Senate shall have the sole Power to try all Impeachments. When sitting for that Purpose, they shall be on Oath or Affirmation. When the President of the United States is tried, the Chief Justice shall preside: And no Person shall be convicted without the Concurrence of two thirds of the Members present.

Judgment in Cases of Impeachment shall not extend further than to removal from Office, and disqualification to hold and enjoy any Office of honor, Trust or Profit under the United States: but the Party convicted shall nevertheless be liable and subject to Indictment, Trial, Judgment and Punishment, according to Law.

Section. 4. The Times, Places and Manner of holding Elections for Senators and Representatives, shall be prescribed in each State by the Legislature thereof; but the Congress may at any time by Law make or alter such Regulations, except as to the Places of chusing Senators.

The Congress shall assemble at least once in every Year, *and such Meeting shall be on the first Monday in December,* unless they shall by Law appoint a different Day.

Section. 5. Each House shall be the Judge of the Elections, Returns and Qualifications of its own Members, and a Majority of each shall constitute a Quorum to do Business; but a smaller

Number may adjourn from day to day, and may be authorized to compel the Attendance of absent Members, in such Manner, and under such Penalties as each House may provide.

Each House may determine the Rules of its Proceedings, punish its Members for disorderly Behaviour, and, with the Concurrence of two thirds, expel a Member.

Each House shall keep a Journal of its Proceedings, and from time to time publish the same, excepting such Parts as may in their Judgment require Secrecy; and the Yeas and Nays of the Members of either House on any question shall, at the Desire of one fifth of those Present, be entered on the Journal.

Neither House, during the Session of Congress, shall, without the Consent of the other, adjourn for more than three days, nor to any other Place than that in which the two Houses shall be sitting.

Section. 6. The Senators and Representatives shall receive a Compensation for their Services, to be ascertained by Law, and paid out of the Treasury of the United States. They shall in all Cases, except Treason, Felony and Breach of the Peace, be privileged from Arrest during their Attendance at the Session of their respective Houses, and in going to and returning from the same; and for any Speech or Debate in either House, they shall not be questioned in any other Place.

No Senator or Representative shall, during the Time for which he was elected, be appointed to any civil Office under the Authority of the United States, which shall have been created, or the Emoluments whereof shall have been encreased during such time; and no Person holding any Office under the United States, shall be a Member of either House during his Continuance in Office.

Section. 7. All Bills for raising Revenue shall originate in the House of Representatives; but the Senate may propose or concur with Amendments as on other Bills.

Every Bill which shall have passed the House of Representatives and the Senate, shall, before it become a Law, be presented to the President of the United States; If he approve he shall sign it, but if not he shall return it, with his Objections to that House in which it shall have originated, who shall enter the Objections at large on their Journal, and proceed to reconsider it. If after such Reconsideration two thirds of that House shall agree to pass the Bill, it shall be sent, together with the Objections, to the other House, by which it shall likewise be reconsidered, and if approved by two thirds of that House, it shall become a Law. But in all such Cases the Votes of both Houses shall be determined by yeas and Nays, and the Names of the Persons voting for and against the Bill shall be entered on the Journal of each House respectively. If any Bill shall not be returned by the President within ten Days (Sundays excepted) after it shall have been presented to him, the Same shall be a Law, in like Manner as if he had signed it, unless the Congress by their Adjournment prevent its Return, in which Case it shall not be a Law.

Every Order, Resolution, or Vote to which the Concurrence of the Senate and House of Representatives may be necessary (except on a question of Adjournment) shall be presented to the President of the United States; and before the Same shall take Effect, shall be approved by him, or being disapproved by him, shall be repassed by two thirds of the Senate and House of Representatives, according to the Rules and Limitations prescribed in the Case of a Bill.

Section. 8. The Congress shall have Power To lay and collect Taxes, Duties, Imposts and Excises, to pay the Debts and provide for the common Defence and general Welfare of the United States; but all Duties, Imposts and Excises shall be uniform throughout the United States;

To borrow Money on the credit of the United States;

To regulate Commerce with foreign Nations, and among the several States, and with the Indian Tribes;

To establish an uniform Rule of Naturalization, and uniform

Laws on the subject of Bankruptcies throughout the United States;

To coin Money, regulate the Value thereof, and of foreign Coin, and fix the Standard of Weights and Measures;

To provide for the Punishment of counterfeiting the Securities and current Coin of the United States;

To establish Post Offices and post Roads;

To promote the Progress of Science and useful Arts, by securing for limited Times to Authors and Inventors the exclusive Right to their respective Writings and Discoveries;

To constitute Tribunals inferior to the supreme Court;

To define and punish Piracies and Felonies committed on the high Seas, and Offences against the Law of Nations;

To declare War, grant Letters of Marque and Reprisal, and make Rules concerning Captures on Land and Water;

To raise and support Armies, but no Appropriation of Money to that Use shall be for a longer Term than two Years;

To provide and maintain a Navy;

To make Rules for the Government and Regulation of the land and naval Forces;

To provide for calling forth the Militia to execute the Laws of the Union, suppress Insurrections and repel Invasions;

To provide for organizing, arming, and disciplining, the Militia, and for governing such Part of them as may be employed in the Service of the United States, reserving to the States respectively, the Appointment of the Officers, and the Authority of training the Militia according to the discipline prescribed by Congress;

To exercise exclusive Legislation in all Cases whatsoever, over such District (not exceeding ten Miles square) as may, by Cession of particular States, and the Acceptance of Congress, become the Seat of the Government of the United States, and to exercise like Authority over all Places purchased by the Consent of the Legislature of the State in which the Same shall be, for the Erection of

Forts, Magazines, Arsenals, dock-Yards, and other needful Buildings;—And To make all Laws which shall be necessary and proper for carrying into Execution the foregoing Powers, and all other Powers vested by this Constitution in the Government of the United States, or in any Department or Officer thereof.

Section. 9. The Migration or Importation of such Persons as any of the States now existing shall think proper to admit, shall not be prohibited by the Congress prior to the Year one thousand eight hundred and eight, but a Tax or duty may be imposed on such Importation, not exceeding ten dollars for each Person.

The Privilege of the Writ of Habeas Corpus shall not be suspended, unless when in Cases of Rebellion or Invasion the public Safety may require it.

No Bill of Attainder or ex post facto Law shall be passed.

No Capitation, or other direct, Tax shall be laid, unless in Proportion to the Census or Enumeration herein before directed to be taken.

No Tax or Duty shall be laid on Articles exported from any State.

No Preference shall be given by any Regulation of Commerce or Revenue to the Ports of one State over those of another; nor shall Vessels bound to, or from, one State, be obliged to enter, clear, or pay Duties in another.

No Money shall be drawn from the Treasury, but in Consequence of Appropriations made by Law; and a regular Statement and Account of the Receipts and Expenditures of all public Money shall be published from time to time.

No Title of Nobility shall be granted by the United States: And no Person holding any Office of Profit or Trust under them, shall, without the Consent of the Congress, accept of any present, Emolument, Office, or Title, of any kind whatever, from any King, Prince, or foreign State.

Section. 10. No State shall enter into any Treaty, Alliance, or Confederation; grant Letters of Marque and Reprisal; coin

Money; emit Bills of Credit; make any Thing but gold and silver Coin a Tender in Payment of Debts; pass any Bill of Attainder, ex post facto Law, or Law impairing the Obligation of Contracts, or grant any Title of Nobility.

No State shall, without the Consent of the Congress, lay any Imposts or Duties on Imports or Exports, except what may be absolutely necessary for executing it's inspection Laws; and the net Produce of all Duties and Imposts, laid by any State on Imports or Exports, shall be for the Use of the Treasury of the United States; and all such Laws shall be subject to the Revision and Controul of the Congress.

No State shall, without the Consent of Congress, lay any Duty of Tonnage, keep Troops, or Ships of War in time of Peace, enter into any Agreement or Compact with another State, or with a foreign Power, or engage in War, unless actually invaded, or in such imminent Danger as will not admit of delay.

ARTICLE. II.

Section. 1. The executive Power shall be vested in a President of the United States of America. He shall hold his Office during the Term of four Years, and, together with the Vice President, chosen for the same Term, be elected, as follows:

Each State shall appoint, in such Manner as the Legislature thereof may direct, a Number of Electors, equal to the whole Number of Senators and Representatives to which the State may be entitled in the Congress: but no Senator or Representative, or Person holding an Office of Trust or Profit under the United States, shall be appointed an Elector.

The Electors shall meet in their respective States, and vote by Ballot for two Persons, of whom one at least shall not be an Inhabitant of the same State with themselves. And they shall make a List of all the Persons voted for, and of the Number of Votes for each; which List they shall sign and certify, and transmit sealed to the Seat of the Government of the United States, directed to the President of the Senate. The President of the Senate shall, in the Presence of the Senate and House of Representatives, open all the Certificates, and the Votes shall then be counted. The Person having the greatest Number of Votes shall be the President, if such Number be a Majority of the whole Number of Electors appointed; and if there be more than one who have such Majority, and have an equal Number of Votes, then the House of Representatives shall immediately chuse by Ballot one of them for President; and if no Person have a Majority, then from the five highest on the List the said House shall in like Manner chuse the President. But in chusing the President, the Votes shall be taken by States, the Representation from each State having one Vote; a quorum for this Purpose shall consist of a Member or Members from two thirds of the States, and a Majority of all the States shall be necessary to a Choice. In every Case, after the Choice of the President, the Person having the greatest Number of Votes of the Electors shall be the Vice President. But if there should remain two or more who have equal Votes, the Senate shall chuse from them by Ballot the Vice President.

The Congress may determine the Time of chusing the Electors, and the Day on which they shall give their Votes; which Day shall be the same throughout the United States.

No Person except a natural born Citizen, or a Citizen of the United States, at the time of the Adoption of this Constitution, shall be eligible to the Office of President; neither shall any Person be eligible to that Office who shall not have attained to the Age of thirty five Years, and been fourteen Years a Resident within the United States.

In Case of the Removal of the President from Office, or of his Death, Resignation, or Inability to discharge the Powers and Duties of the said Office, the Same shall devolve on the Vice President, and the Congress may by Law provide for the Case of Removal, Death, Resignation or Inability, both of the President and Vice President, declaring what Officer shall then act as President, and such Officer shall act accordingly, until the Disability be removed, or a President shall be elected.

The President shall, at stated Times, receive for his Services, a Compensation, which shall neither be increased nor diminished during the Period for which he shall have been elected, and he shall not receive within that Period any other Emolument from the United States, or any of them.

Before he enter on the Execution of his Office, he shall take the following Oath or Affirmation:—"I do solemnly swear (or affirm) that I will faithfully execute the Office of President of the United States, and will to the best of my Ability, preserve, protect and defend the Constitution of the United States."

Section. 2. The President shall be Commander in Chief of the Army and Navy of the United States, and of the Militia of the several States, when called into the actual Service of the United States; he may require the Opinion, in writing, of the principal Officer in each of the executive Departments, upon any Subject relating to the Duties of their respective Offices, and he shall have Power to grant Reprieves and Pardons for Offences against the United States, except in Cases of Impeachment.

He shall have Power, by and with the Advice and Consent of the Senate, to make Treaties, provided two thirds of the Senators present concur; and he shall nominate, and by and with the Advice and Consent of the Senate, shall appoint Ambassadors, other public Ministers and Consuls, Judges of the supreme Court, and all other Officers of the United States, whose Appointments are not herein otherwise provided for, and which shall be established by Law: but the Congress may by Law vest the Appointment of such inferior Officers, as they think proper, in the President alone, in the Courts of Law, or in the Heads of Departments.

The President shall have Power to fill up all Vacancies that may happen during the Recess of the Senate, by granting Commissions which shall expire at the End of their next Session.

Section. 3. He shall from time to time give to the Congress Information of the State of the Union, and recommend to their Consideration such Measures as he shall judge necessary and expedient; he may, on extraordinary Occasions, convene both Houses, or either of them, and in Case of Disagreement between them, with Respect to the Time of Adjournment, he may adjourn them to such Time as he shall think proper; he shall receive Ambassadors and other public Ministers; he shall take Care that the Laws be faithfully executed, and shall Commission all the Officers of the United States.

Section. 4. The President, Vice President and all civil Officers of the United States, shall be removed from Office on Impeachment for, and Conviction of, Treason, Bribery, or other high Crimes and Misdemeanors.

ARTICLE. III.

Section. 1. The judicial Power of the United States shall be vested in one supreme Court, and in such inferior Courts as the Congress may from time to time ordain and establish. The Judges, both of the supreme and inferior Courts, shall hold their Offices during good Behaviour, and shall, at stated Times, receive for their Services a Compensation, which shall not be diminished during their Continuance in Office.

Section. 2. The judicial Power shall extend to all Cases, in Law and Equity, arising under this Constitution, the Laws of the United States, and Treaties made, or which shall be made, under their Authority;—to all Cases affecting Ambassadors, other public Ministers and Consuls;—to all Cases of admiralty and maritime Jurisdiction;—to Controversies to which the United States shall be a Party;—to Controversies between two or more States;—between a State and Citizens of another State;—between Citizens of different States;—between Citizens of the same State claiming Lands under Grants of different States, and between a State, or the Citizens thereof, and foreign States, Citizens or Subjects.

In all Cases affecting Ambassadors, other public Ministers

and Consuls, and those in which a State shall be Party, the supreme Court shall have original Jurisdiction. In all the other Cases before mentioned, the supreme Court shall have appellate Jurisdiction, both as to Law and Fact, with such Exceptions, and under such Regulations as the Congress shall make.

The Trial of all Crimes, except in Cases of Impeachment, shall be by Jury; and such Trial shall be held in the State where the said Crimes shall have been committed; but when not committed within any State, the Trial shall be at such Place or Places as the Congress may by Law have directed.

Section. 3. Treason against the United States shall consist only in levying War against them, or in adhering to their Enemies, giving them Aid and Comfort. No Person shall be convicted of Treason unless on the Testimony of two Witnesses to the same overt Act, or on Confession in open Court.

The Congress shall have Power to declare the Punishment of Treason, but no Attainder of Treason shall work Corruption of Blood, or Forfeiture except during the Life of the Person attainted.

ARTICLE. IV.

Section. 1. Full Faith and Credit shall be given in each State to the public Acts, Records, and judicial Proceedings of every other State. And the Congress may by general Laws prescribe the Manner in which such Acts, Records and Proceedings shall be proved, and the Effect thereof.

Section. 2. The Citizens of each State shall be entitled to all Privileges and Immunities of Citizens in the several States.

A Person charged in any State with Treason, Felony, or other Crime, who shall flee from Justice, and be found in another State, shall on Demand of the executive Authority of the State from which he fled, be delivered up, to be removed to the State having Jurisdiction of the Crime.

No Person held to Service or Labour in one State, under the Laws thereof, escaping into another, shall, in Consequence of any

Law or Regulation therein, be discharged from such Service or Labour, but shall be delivered up on Claim of the Party to whom such Service or Labour may be due.

Section. 3. New States may be admitted by the Congress into this Union; but no new State shall be formed or erected within the Jurisdiction of any other State; nor any State be formed by the Junction of two or more States, or Parts of States, without the Consent of the Legislatures of the States concerned as well as of the Congress.

The Congress shall have Power to dispose of and make all needful Rules and Regulations respecting the Territory or other Property belonging to the United States; and nothing in this Constitution shall be so construed as to Prejudice any Claims of the United States, or of any particular State.

Section. 4. The United States shall guarantee to every State in this Union a Republican Form of Government, and shall protect each of them against Invasion; and on Application of the Legislature, or of the Executive (when the Legislature cannot be convened), against domestic Violence.

ARTICLE. V.

The Congress, whenever two thirds of both Houses shall deem it necessary, shall propose Amendments to this Constitution, or, on the Application of the Legislatures of two thirds of the several States, shall call a Convention for proposing Amendments, which, in either Case, shall be valid to all Intents and Purposes, as Part of this Constitution, when ratified by the Legislatures of three fourths of the several States, or by Conventions in three fourths thereof, as the one or the other Mode of Ratification may be proposed by the Congress; Provided that no Amendment which may be made prior to the Year One thousand eight hundred and eight shall in any Manner affect the first and fourth Clauses in the Ninth Section of the first Article; and that no State, without its Consent, shall be deprived of its equal Suffrage in the Senate.

ARTICLE. VI.

All Debts contracted and Engagements entered into, before the Adoption of this Constitution, shall be as valid against the United States under this Constitution, as under the Confederation. This Constitution, and the Laws of the United States which shall be made in Pursuance thereof; and all Treaties made, or which shall be made, under the Authority of the United States, shall be the supreme Law of the Land; and the Judges in every State shall be bound thereby, any Thing in the Constitution or Laws of any State to the Contrary notwithstanding.

The Senators and Representatives before mentioned, and the Members of the several State Legislatures, and all executive and judicial Officers, both of the United States and of the several States, shall be bound by Oath or Affirmation, to support this Constitution; but no religious Test shall ever be required as a Qualification to any Office or public Trust under the United States.

ARTICLE. VII.

The Ratification of the Conventions of nine States, shall be sufficient for the Establishment of this Constitution between the States so ratifying the Same.

The Word, "the," being interlined between the seventh and eighth Lines of the first Page, The Word "Thirty" being partly written on an Erazure in the fifteenth Line of the first Page, The Words "is tried" being interlined between the thirty second and thirty third Lines of the first Page and the Word "the" being interlined between the forty third and forty fourth Lines of the second Page.

Attest WILLIAM JACKSON
Secretary
done in Convention by the Unanimous Consent of the States present the Seventeenth Day of September in the Year of our

Lord one thousand seven hundred and Eighty seven and of the Independence of the United States of America the Twelfth[.] In witness whereof We have hereunto subscribed our Names,

Go. WASHINGTON—Presidt.
and deputy from Virginia

New Hampshire { John Langdon
Nicholas Gilman

Massachusetts { Nathaniel Gorham
Rufus King

Connecticut { Wm. Saml. Johnson
Roger Sherman

New York . . . Alexander Hamilton

New Jersey { Wil: Livingston
David Brearley
Wm. Paterson
Jona: Dayton

Pennsylvania { B Franklin
Thomas Mifflin
Robt Morris
Geo. Clymer
Thos. Fitz Simons
Jared Ingersoll
James Wilson
Gouv Morris

Delaware { Geo: Read
Gunning Bedford jun
John Dickinson
Richard Bassett
Jaco: Broom

Maryland { James McHenry
Dan of St Thos. Jenifer
Danl Carroll

Virginia { John Blair
James Madison jr

North Carolina { Wm. Blount
Richd. Dobbs Spaight
Hu Williamson

South Carolina { J. Rutledge
Charles Cotesworth Pinckney
Charles Pinckney
Pierce Butler

Georgia { William Few
Abr Baldwin

IN CONVENTION MONDAY, SEPTEMBER 17TH, 1787.

Present

The States of New-Hampshire, Massachusetts, Connecticut, MR. *Hamilton* from New-York, New Jersey, Pennsylvania, Delaware, Maryland, Virginia, North Carolina, South Carolina and Georgia. Resolved,

That the preceeding Constitution be laid before the United States in Congress assembled, and that it is the Opinion of this Convention, that it should afterwards be submitted to a Convention of Delegates, chosen in each State by the People thereof, under the Recommendation of its Legislature, for their Assent and Ratification; and that each Convention assenting to, and ratifying the Same, should give Notice thereof to the United States in Congress assembled. Resolved, That it is the Opinion of this

Convention, that as soon as the Conventions of nine States shall have ratified this Constitution, the United States in Congress assembled should fix a Day on which Electors should be appointed by the States which have ratified the same, and a Day on which the Electors should assemble to vote for the President, and the Time and Place for commencing Proceedings under this Constitution. That after such Publication the Electors should be appointed, and the Senators and Representatives elected: That the Electors should meet on the Day fixed for the Election of the President, and should transmit their Votes certified, signed, sealed and directed, as the Constitution requires, to the Secretary of the United States in Congress assembled, that the Senators and Representatives should convene at the Time and Place assigned; that the Senators should appoint a President of the Senate, for the sole purpose of receiving, opening and counting the Votes for President; and, that after he shall be chosen, the Congress, together with the President, should, without Delay, proceed to execute this Constitution.

By the Unanimous Order of the Convention
Go. WASHINGTON—Presidt.
W. JACKSON Secretary.

AMENDMENT 1

Congress shall make no law respecting an establishment of religion, or prohibiting the free exercise thereof; or abridging the freedom of speech, or of the press; or the right of the people peaceably to assemble, and to petition the Government for a redress of grievances.

AMENDMENT 2

A well regulated Militia, being necessary to the security of a free State, the right of the people to keep and bear Arms, shall not be infringed.

AMENDMENT 3

No Soldier shall, in time of peace be quartered in any house, without the consent of the Owner, nor in time of war, but in a manner to be prescribed by law.

AMENDMENT 4

The right of the people to be secure in their persons, houses, papers, and effects, against unreasonable searches and seizures, shall not be violated, and no Warrants shall issue, but upon probable cause, supported by Oath or affirmation, and particularly describing the place to be searched, and the persons or things to be seized.

AMENDMENT 5

No person shall be held to answer for a capital, or otherwise infamous crime, unless on a presentment or indictment of a Grand Jury, except in cases arising in the land or naval forces, or in the Militia, when in actual service in time of War or public danger; nor shall any person be subject for the same offense to be twice put in jeopardy of life or limb; nor shall be compelled in any criminal case to be a witness against himself, nor be deprived of life, liberty, or property, without due process of law; nor shall private property be taken for public use, without just compensation.

AMENDMENT 6

In all criminal prosecutions, the accused shall enjoy the right to a speedy and public trial, by an impartial jury of the State and district wherein the crime shall have been committed, which district shall have been previously ascertained by law, and to be informed of the nature and cause of the accusation; to be confronted with the witnesses against him; to have compulsory process for obtaining witnesses in his favor, and to have the Assistance of Counsel for his defence.

AMENDMENT 7

In Suits at common law, where the value in controversy shall exceed twenty dollars, the right of trial by jury shall be preserved, and no fact tried by a jury, shall be otherwise re-examined in any Court of the United States, than according to the rules of the common law.

AMENDMENT 8

Excessive bail shall not be required, nor excessive fines imposed, nor cruel and unusual punishments inflicted.

AMENDMENT 9

The enumeration in the Constitution, of certain rights, shall not be construed to deny or disparage others retained by the people.

AMENDMENT 10

The powers not delegated to the United States by the Constitution, nor prohibited by it to the States, are reserved to the States respectively, or to the people.

AMENDMENT 11

The Judicial power of the United States shall not be construed to extend to any suit in law or equity, commenced or prosecuted against one of the United States by Citizens of another State, or by Citizens or Subjects of any Foreign State.

AMENDMENT 12

The Electors shall meet in their respective states, and vote by ballot for President and Vice-President, one of whom, at least, shall not be an inhabitant of the same state with themselves; they shall name in their ballots the person voted for as President, and in distinct ballots the person voted for as Vice-President, and they shall make distinct lists of all persons voted for as President, and of all persons voted for as Vice-President and of the number of votes for each, which lists they shall sign and certify, and transmit sealed to the seat of the government of the United States, directed to the President of the Senate;

The President of the Senate shall, in the presence of the Senate and House of Representatives, open all the certificates and the votes shall then be counted;

The person having the greatest Number of votes for President, shall be the President, if such number be a majority of the whole number of Electors appointed; and if no person have such majority, then from the persons having the highest numbers not exceeding three on the list of those voted for as President, the House of Representatives shall choose immediately, by ballot, the President. But in choosing the President, the votes shall be taken by states, the representation from each state having one vote; a quorum for this purpose shall consist of a member or members from two-thirds of the states, and a majority of all the states shall be necessary to a choice. And if the House of Representatives shall not choose a President whenever the right of choice shall devolve upon them, before the fourth day of March next following, then the Vice-President shall act as President, as in the case of the death or other constitutional disability of the President.

The person having the greatest number of votes as Vice-President, shall be the Vice-President, if such number be a majority of the whole number of Electors appointed, and if no person have a majority, then from the two highest numbers on the list, the Senate shall choose the Vice-President; a quorum for the purpose shall consist of two-thirds of the whole number of Senators, and a majority of the whole number shall be necessary to a choice. But no person constitutionally ineligible to the office of President shall be eligible to that of Vice-President of the United States.

AMENDMENT 13

1. Neither slavery nor involuntary servitude, except as a punishment for crime whereof the party shall have been duly convicted,

shall exist within the United States, or any place subject to their jurisdiction.

2. Congress shall have power to enforce this article by appropriate legislation.

AMENDMENT 14

1. All persons born or naturalized in the United States, and subject to the jurisdiction thereof, are citizens of the United States and of the State wherein they reside. No State shall make or enforce any law which shall abridge the privileges or immunities of citizens of the United States; nor shall any State deprive any person of life, liberty, or property, without due process of law; nor deny to any person within its jurisdiction the equal protection of the laws.

2. Representatives shall be apportioned among the several States according to their respective numbers, counting the whole number of persons in each State, excluding Indians not taxed. But when the right to vote at any election for the choice of electors for President and Vice-President of the United States, Representatives in Congress, the Executive and Judicial officers of a State, or the members of the Legislature thereof, is denied to any of the male inhabitants of such State, being twenty-one years of age, and citizens of the United States, or in any way abridged, except for participation in rebellion, or other crime, the basis of representation therein shall be reduced in the proportion which the number of such male citizens shall bear to the whole number of male citizens twenty-one years of age in such State.

3. No person shall be a Senator or Representative in Congress, or elector of President and Vice-President, or hold any office, civil or military, under the United States, or under any State, who, having previously taken an oath, as a member of Congress, or as an officer of the United States, or as a member of any State legislature, or as an executive or judicial officer of any State, to support the Constitution of the United States, shall have engaged

in insurrection or rebellion against the same, or given aid or comfort to the enemies thereof. But Congress may by a vote of two-thirds of each House, remove such disability.

4. The validity of the public debt of the United States, authorized by law, including debts incurred for payment of pensions and bounties for services in suppressing insurrection or rebellion, shall not be questioned. But neither the United States nor any State shall assume or pay any debt or obligation incurred in aid of insurrection or rebellion against the United States, or any claim for the loss or emancipation of any slave; but all such debts, obligations and claims shall be held illegal and void.

5. The Congress shall have power to enforce, by appropriate legislation, the provisions of this article.

AMENDMENT 15

1. The right of citizens of the United States to vote shall not be denied or abridged by the United States or by any State on account of race, color, or previous condition of servitude.

2. The Congress shall have power to enforce this article by appropriate legislation.

AMENDMENT 16

The Congress shall have power to lay and collect taxes on incomes, from whatever source derived, without apportionment among the several States, and without regard to any census or enumeration.

AMENDMENT 17

The Senate of the United States shall be composed of two Senators from each State, elected by the people thereof, for six years; and each Senator shall have one vote. The electors in each State shall have the qualifications requisite for electors of the most numerous branch of the State legislatures.

When vacancies happen in the representation of any State in

the Senate, the executive authority of such State shall issue writs of election to fill such vacancies: Provided, That the legislature of any State may empower the executive thereof to make temporary appointments until the people fill the vacancies by election as the legislature may direct.

This amendment shall not be so construed as to affect the election or term of any Senator chosen before it becomes valid as part of the Constitution.

AMENDMENT 18

1. After one year from the ratification of this article the manufacture, sale, or transportation of intoxicating liquors within, the importation thereof into, or the exportation thereof from the United States and all territory subject to the jurisdiction thereof for beverage purposes is hereby prohibited.

2. The Congress and the several States shall have concurrent power to enforce this article by appropriate legislation.

3. This article shall be inoperative unless it shall have been ratified as an amendment to the Constitution by the legislatures of the several States, as provided in the Constitution, within seven years from the date of the submission hereof to the States by the Congress.

AMENDMENT 19

The right of citizens of the United States to vote shall not be denied or abridged by the United States or by any State on account of sex.

Congress shall have power to enforce this article by appropriate legislation.

AMENDMENT 20

1. The terms of the President and Vice President shall end at noon on the 20th day of January, and the terms of Senators and Representatives at noon on the 3rd day of January, of the years

in which such terms would have ended if this article had not been ratified; and the terms of their successors shall then begin.

2. The Congress shall assemble at least once in every year, and such meeting shall begin at noon on the 3d day of January, unless they shall by law appoint a different day.

3. If, at the time fixed for the beginning of the term of the President, the President elect shall have died, the Vice President elect shall become President. If a President shall not have been chosen before the time fixed for the beginning of his term, or if the President elect shall have failed to qualify, then the Vice President elect shall act as President until a President shall have qualified; and the Congress may by law provide for the case wherein neither a President elect nor a Vice President elect shall have qualified, declaring who shall then act as President, or the manner in which one who is to act shall be selected, and such person shall act accordingly until a President or Vice President shall have qualified.

4. The Congress may by law provide for the case of the death of any of the persons from whom the House of Representatives may choose a President whenever the right of choice shall have devolved upon them, and for the case of the death of any of the persons from whom the Senate may choose a Vice President whenever the right of choice shall have devolved upon them.

5. Sections 1 and 2 shall take effect on the 15th day of October following the ratification of this article.

6. This article shall be inoperative unless it shall have been ratified as an amendment to the Constitution by the legislatures of three-fourths of the several States within seven years from the date of its submission.

AMENDMENT 21

1. The eighteenth article of amendment to the Constitution of the United States is hereby repealed.

2. The transportation or importation into any State, Territory, or possession of the United States for delivery or use therein

of intoxicating liquors, in violation of the laws thereof, is hereby prohibited.

3. The article shall be inoperative unless it shall have been ratified as an amendment to the Constitution by conventions in the several States, as provided in the Constitution, within seven years from the date of the submission hereof to the States by the Congress.

AMENDMENT 22

1. No person shall be elected to the office of the President more than twice, and no person who has held the office of President, or acted as President, for more than two years of a term to which some other person was elected President shall be elected to the office of the President more than once. But this Article shall not apply to any person holding the office of President, when this Article was proposed by the Congress, and shall not prevent any person who may be holding the office of President, or acting as President, during the term within which this Article becomes operative from holding the office of President or acting as President during the remainder of such term.

2. This article shall be inoperative unless it shall have been ratified as an amendment to the Constitution by the legislatures of three-fourths of the several States within seven years from the date of its submission to the States by the Congress.

AMENDMENT 23

1. The District constituting the seat of Government of the United States shall appoint in such manner as the Congress may direct: A number of electors of President and Vice President equal to the whole number of Senators and Representatives in Congress to which the District would be entitled if it were a State, but in no event more than the least populous State; they shall be in addition to those appointed by the States, but they shall be considered, for the purposes of the election of President and Vice

President, to be electors appointed by a State; and they shall meet in the District and perform such duties as provided by the twelfth article of amendment.

2. The Congress shall have power to enforce this article by appropriate legislation.

AMENDMENT 24

1. The right of citizens of the United States to vote in any primary or other election for President or Vice President, for electors for President or Vice President, or for Senator or Representative in Congress, shall not be denied or abridged by the United States or any State by reason of failure to pay any poll tax or other tax.

2. The Congress shall have power to enforce this article by appropriate legislation.

AMENDMENT 25

1. In case of the removal of the President from office or of his death or resignation, the Vice President shall become President.

2. Whenever there is a vacancy in the office of the Vice President, the President shall nominate a Vice President who shall take office upon confirmation by a majority vote of both Houses of Congress.

3. Whenever the President transmits to the President pro tempore of the Senate and the Speaker of the House of Representatives his written declaration that he is unable to discharge the powers and duties of his office, and until he transmits to them a written declaration to the contrary, such powers and duties shall be discharged by the Vice President as Acting President.

4. Whenever the Vice President and a majority of either the principal officers of the executive departments or of such other body as Congress may by law provide, transmit to the President pro tempore of the Senate and the Speaker of the House of Representatives their written declaration that the President is unable

to discharge the powers and duties of his office, the Vice President shall immediately assume the powers and duties of the office as Acting President.

Thereafter, when the President transmits to the President pro tempore of the Senate and the Speaker of the House of Representatives his written declaration that no inability exists, he shall resume the powers and duties of his office unless the Vice President and a majority of either the principal officers of the executive department or of such other body as Congress may by law provide, transmit within four days to the President pro tempore of the Senate and the Speaker of the House of Representatives their written declaration that the President is unable to discharge the powers and duties of his office. Thereupon Congress shall decide the issue, assembling within forty eight hours for that purpose if not in session. If the Congress, within twenty one days after receipt of the latter written declaration, or, if Congress is not in session, within twenty one days after Congress is required to assemble, determines by two thirds vote of both Houses that the President is unable to discharge the powers and duties of his office, the Vice President shall continue to discharge the same as Acting President; otherwise, the President shall resume the powers and duties of his office.

AMENDMENT 26

1. The right of citizens of the United States, who are eighteen years of age or older, to vote shall not be denied or abridged by the United States or by any State on account of age.

2. The Congress shall have power to enforce this article by appropriate legislation.

AMENDMENT 27

No law, varying the compensation for the services of the Senators and Representatives, shall take effect, until an election of Representatives shall have intervened.

NOTES

———//———

INTRODUCTION

1. Richard Beeman, *Plain, Honest Men: The Making of the American Constitution* (New York: Random House, 2009), p. 106.
2. Jesse Lee, "The President's Remarks on Justice Souter," (2009), available at http://www.whitehouse.gov/blog/09/05/01/The-Presidents-Remarks-on -Justice-Souter.
3. Gerhard Casper and Richard A. Posner, *The Workload of the Supreme Court* (Chicago: American Bar Foundation, 1976), p. 16.
4. Stephen M. Shapiro, "Oral Argument in the Supreme Court: The Felt Necessities of the Time," in *Yearbook of the Supreme Court History Society 1985*, p. 22.
5. Charles Warren, *The Supreme Court in United States History*, vol. 1 (Boston: Little, Brown, 1923), p. 471.
6. Shapiro, "Oral Argument in the Supreme Court," pp. 23, 29.

LOOMING LARGE
Historic Intersections of the President and the Supreme Court

1. Thomas Jefferson to William Johnson, June 12, 1823, available at http:// www.let.rug.nl/usa/P/tj3/writings/brf/jefl272.htm.
2. Thomas Jefferson to John Tyler, May 26, 1810, available at http://www.let .rug.nl/usa/P/tj3/writings/brf/jefl205.htm.

3. Thomas Jefferson to Thomas Ritchie, Dec. 25, 1820, available at http://www.let.rug.nl/usa/P/tj3/writings/brf/jefl263.htm.

4. Joseph J. Ellis, *American Sphinx: The Character of Thomas Jefferson* (New York: Knopf, 1997), p. 176.

5. Ibid., p. 175.

6. *Marbury v. Madison*, 1 Cranch 137, 177, 180 (1803).

7. *Ex parte Merryman*, 17 F. Cas. 144, 153 (C.C.D. Md. 1861).

8. Abraham Lincoln, "Message to Congress in Special Session" (1861), in *Abraham Lincoln: Speeches and Writings, 1859–1865* (New York: Library of America, 1989), p. 253.

9. Abraham Lincoln, "Speech at Edwardsville," Sept. 11, 1854, in *The Collected Works of Abraham Lincoln: 1858–1860*, Vol. 3 (New Brunswick, NJ: Rutgers University Press, 1953), p. 91.

10. *Youngstown Sheet & Tube v. Sawyer*, 343 U.S. 579 (1952).

11. Ken Gormley, "Foreword: President Truman and the Steel Seizure Case: A Symposium," *Duquesne Law Review* 41 (2003), pp. 675–76.

12. Id. at 676.

13. *Hamdi v. Rumsfeld*, 542 U.S. 507, 532 (2004).

14. Id. at 536.

15. Ibid.

16. *Hamdan v. Rumsfeld*, 548 U.S. 557, 630 (2006).

17. *Boumediene v. Bush*, 553 U.S. 723, 798 (2008).

THE CALL TO SERVE
Judicial Appointments

1. *Marbury v. Madison*, 1 Cranch 137 (1803).

2. *McCulloch v. Maryland*, 4 Wheat. 316 (1819).

3. R. Kent Newmyer, "A Note on the Whig Politics of Justice Joseph Story," *Mississippi Valley Historical Review* 48 (1961), p. 482.

4. Thomas Jefferson to Thomas Ritchie, Dec. 25, 1820, available at http://www.let.rug.nl/usa/P/tj3/writings/brf/jefl263.htm.

5. *Dred Scott v. Sanford*, 19 How. 393 (1857).

6. *Selections from the Correspondence of Theodore Roosevelt and Henry Cabot Lodge: 1884–1918* (New York: Charles Scribner's Sons, 1925), p. 519.

7. Charles P. Curtis, *Lions Under the Throne* (Boston: Houghton Mifflin, 1947), p. 281.

8. Alpheus Thomas Mason, *William Howard Taft, Chief Justice* (New York: Simon & Schuster, 1965), p. 39.

9. *Palko v. Connecticut*, 302 U.S. 319 (1937).

10. *West Coast Hotel v. Parrish*, 300 U.S. 379 (1937).

11. *Brown v. Board of Education*, 347 U.S. 483 (1954).

12. *Reynolds v. Simms*, 377 U.S. 533 (1964).

13. *Miranda v. Arizona*, 384 U.S. 436 (1966).

14. Henry J. Abraham, *Justices and Presidents: A Political History of Appointments to the Supreme Court* (New York: Oxford University Press, 1985), p. 263.

15. Juan Williams, *Thurgood Marshall: American Revolutionary* (New York: Times Books, 1998), p. 12.

16. *Brown v. Board of Education*, 347 U.S. 483 (1954).

17. Keith E. Whittington, "Presidents, Senates, and Failed Supreme Court Nominations," *Supreme Court Review 2006*, p. 438.

A HOUSE IS NOT A HOME
The Journey to One First Street

1. Robert P. Reeder, "The First Homes of the Supreme Court of the United States," *Proceedings of the American Philosophical Society* 76 (1936), pp. 545–46.

2. Id. at 548.

3. Leon Friedman and Fred L. Israel, *The Justices of the United States Supreme Court: Their Lives and Major Opinions*, vol. 1 (New York: Chelsea House, 1997), p. 42.

4. Reeder, "The First Homes of the Supreme Court," p. 550.

5. Friedman and Israel, *The Justices*, vol. 1, p. 42.

6. Residence Act of 1790, §§ 1, 5, 6, 1 Stat. 130.

7. Reeder, "The First Homes of the Supreme Court," p. 552.

8. Id. at 575–76.

9. Id. at 577.

10. Id. at 583.

11. Geoffrey Blodgett, "Cass Gilbert, Architect: Conservative at Bay," *Journal of American History* 72 (1985), p. 631.

12. Id. at 618.

13. Arthur Cotton Moore, "A New National Mall for the 21st Century," *Washingtonian*, July 2006.

14. Herbert C. Plummer, "A Washington Daybook," *Evening Independent* (Massillon, Ohio), Feb. 2, 1929.

15. Cass Gilbert Jr., "The United States Supreme Court Building," *Architecture* 72 (1935), p. 301.

16. Jan Crawford Greenburg, *Supreme Conflict: The Inside Story of the Struggle for Control of the United States Supreme Court* (New York: Penguin, 2007), p. 210.

17. Blodgett, "Cass Gilbert, Architect," p. 633.

18. Gilbert Jr., "The United States Supreme Court Building," p. 302.

19. Ibid.

20. Blodgett, "Cass Gilbert, Architect," p. 632.

21. Charles E. Hughes, "An Imperishable Ideal of Liberty Under Law," available at http://c0403731.cdn.cloudfiles.rackspacecloud.com/collection/papers/1930/1932_1013_LibertyHughesT.pdf.

22. Gilbert Jr., "The United States Supreme Court Building," p. 303.

23. Blodgett, "Cass Gilbert, Architect," p. 634.

24. Id. at 634 n.44.

25. Ibid.

26. *Proceedings in Commemoration of the 50th Anniversary of the Opening of the Supreme Court Building*, 474 U.S. v–xxi (Oct. 7, 1985).

27. "Statement Concerning the Supreme Court's Front Entrance, Memorandum of Justice Breyer," *Journal of the Supreme Court of the United States: October Term 2009*, available at http://www.supremecourt.gov/orders/journal/jnl09.pdf, pp. 831–32.

HUMBLE BEGINNINGS
The First Decade of the United States Supreme Court

1. U.S. Const. art. III, §1.

2. Judiciary Act of 1789 §1, 1 Stat. 73

3. Friedman and Israel, *The Justices*, vol. 1, p. 10.

4. Id. at 42.

5. Id. at 65.

6. Id. at 111.

7. Ibid.

8. United States Senate, "Supreme Court Nominations, 1789–Present," available at http://www.senate.gov/pagelayout/reference/nominations/reverseNominations.htm.

9. Friedman and Israel, *The Justices*, vol. 1, p. 127.

10. Id. at 128.

11. Judiciary Act of 1789, 1 Stat. 73.

12. Friedman and Israel, *The Justices*, vol. 1, pp. 32, 42.

13. Id. at 18.

14. Id. at 44–45.

15. Id. at 43.

16. Id. at 45; see also *Independent Chronicle* (Boston), Aug. 13, 1795, in Maeva Marcus and James R. Perry, eds., *The Documentary History of the Supreme Court of the United States, 1789–1800*, vol. 2 (New York: Columbia University Press, 1985), p. 780.

17. Friedman and Israel, *The Justices,* vol. 1, p. 46.

18. Id. at 46.

19. United States Senate, "Supreme Court Nominations, 1789–Present," available at http://www.senate.gov/pagelayout/reference/nominations/reverseNominations.htm.

20. Ibid.

21. Friedman and Israel, *The Justices,* vol. 1, p. 66.

22. Id. at 230.

23. Id. at 233.

24. Id. at 19–20.

25. Marcus and Perry, *The Documentary History of the Supreme Court,* vol. 1, p. 162.

26. Ibid.

27. Gerald T. Dunne, "Early Court Reporters," in *Yearbook of the Supreme Court History Society 1976,* pp. 61, 62.

28. Id. at 62.

29. Id. at 63.

30. Id. at 62–63.

31. Id. at 63.

32. Sandra Day O'Connor, *The Majesty of the Law: Reflections of a Supreme Court Justice* (New York: Random House, 2003), p. 26.

33. Ibid.

34. Dunne, "Early Court Reporters," p. 63.

35. Id. at 64.

36. Id. at 61.

37. *Worcester v. Georgia,* 31 U.S. (6 Pet.) 515 (1832).

38. *See* "Worcester v. Georgia (1832)," in *The New Georgia Encyclopedia,* available at http://www.newgeorgiaencyclopedia.org/nge/Article.jsp?id=h-2720.

39. George Washington to William Cushing, September 30, 1789, in Marcus and Perry, eds., *The Documentary History of the Supreme Court,* vol. 1, p. 29.

ITINERANT JUSTICE
Riding Circuit

1. James Iredell to Timothy Pickering, June 16, 1798, in Marcus and Perry, eds. *The Documentary History of the Supreme Court,* vol. 3, p. 278 (emphasis added).

2. William Paterson, "Notes for Remarks on Judiciary Bill" and "Notes on Judiciary Bill Debate," June 23, 1789, in Marcus and Perry, eds., *The Documentary History of the Supreme Court,* vol. 4, pp. 410–417.

3. William H. Rehnquist, *Grand Inquests: The Historic Impeachments of Justice Samuel Chase and President Andrew Johnson* (New York: Morrow, 1992), pp. 52, 92–93, 104.

4. James Iredell to Hannah Iredell, Sept. 19, 1791, in Marcus and Perry, eds., *The Documentary History of the Supreme Court*, vol. 2, pp. 210.

5. James Iredell to Hannah Iredell, Nov. 11, 1791, in ibid., p. 229.

6. James Iredell to Hannah Iredell, April 27, 1792, in ibid., p. 272.

7. James Iredell to Hannah Iredell, April 10, 1798, in Marcus and Perry, ed., *The Documentary History of the Supreme Court*, vol. 3, p. 245.

8. Thomas Johnson to George Washington, Jan. 16, 1798, in Marcus and Perry, eds., *The Documentary History of the Supreme Court*, vol. 2, p. 344.

9. *Stuart v. Laird*, 1 Cranch 299 (1803).

10. Rehnquist, *Grand Inquests*, pp. 92–93.

11. Id. at 93.

12. Id. at 104.

13. R. Kent Newmyer, "Justice Joseph Story on Circuit and a Neglected Phase of American Legal History," *American Journal of Legal History* 14 (1970), p. 126 (quoting Joseph Story to Joseph Hopkinson, Feb. 16, 1840).

14. Joshua Glick, "On the Road: The Supreme Court and the History of Circuit Riding," *Cardozo Law Review* 24 (2003), p. 1806; see also Felix Frankfurter and James M. Landis, *The Business of the Supreme Court* (New York: Macmillan, 1928), p. 49.

15. Glick, "On The Road," p. 1799 (quoting 33 *Annals of Cong.* 126 [1819]).

16. Id. at 1799 n.338 (quoting 33 *Annals of Cong.* 131–32 [1819]).

17. Id. at 1808–09 (quoting *Cong. Globe Appendix*, 30th Cong., 1st Sess. 642–43 [1848]).

18. Id. at 1809 (quoting *Cong. Globe*, 30th Cong., 1st Sess. 596 [1848]).

19. Erwin N. Griswold, "The Supreme Court, 1959 Term, Forward: Of Time and Attitudes—Professor Hart and Judge Arnold," *Harvard Law Review* 74 (1960), p. 81.

20. See, e.g., John O. McGinnis, "Justice Without Justices," *Constitutional Commentary* 16 (1999), p. 543.

21. See statements by Akhil Amar in Federalist Society, "Relimiting Federal Judicial Power: Should Congress Play a Role?," *Journal of Law & Policy* 13 (1997), pp. 643–44.

22. See McGinnis, "Justice Without Justices," pp. 541–43.

THE SUPREME COURT'S CHANGING JURISDICTION

1. Joan Biskupic, *Sandra Day O'Connor: How the First Woman on the Supreme Court Became Its Most Influential Justice* (New York: Harper Perennial, 2006), p. 104.

2. "Statistics as of July 2, 1982," *Journal of the Supreme Court of the United States: October Term 1981.*

3. Eugene Gressman, Kenneth S. Gellar, Stephen M. Shapiro, Timothy S. Bishop, and Edward A. Hartnett, *Supreme Court Practice,* 9th ed. (Arlington, VA: BNA, 2007), p. 72.

4. Id. at 73.

5. Ibid.; see also Judiciary Act of 1789, 1 Stat. 73.

6. Bennett Boskey and Eugene Gressman, "The Supreme Court Bids Farewell to Mandatory Appeals," *Federal Rules of Decision* 121 (1988), pp. 81–82.

7. Edward A. Hartnett, "Questioning Certiorari: Some Reflections Seventy-Five Years After the Judges' Bill," *Columbia Law Review* 100 (2000), p. 1650.

8. Frankfurter and Landis, *The Business of the Supreme Court,* p. 257.

9. Act of March 3, 1891, 26 Stat. 826.

10. Gressman et al., *Supreme Court Practice,* p. 75.

11. William H. Rehnquist, *The Supreme Court* (New York: Knopf, 2001), pp. 236–38.

12. William H. Taft, "The Attacks on the Courts and Legal Procedure," *Kentucky Law Review* 5 (1916), p. 18.

13. Byron R. White, "Challenges for the U.S. Supreme Court and the Bar," *Antitrust Law Journal* 51 (1982), p. 282.

14. Hartnett, "Questioning Certiorari," p. 1662.

15. Id. at 1663.

16. Id. at 1648, 1697.

17. Id. at 1643.

18. Rehnquist, *The Supreme Court,* pp. 236–37.

19. Judicial Improvements And Access To Justice Act, Pub. L. No. 100–702, 102 Stat. 4642 (1988).

20. Boskey and Gressman, "Farewell To Mandatory Appeals," p. 81.

21. *Dick v. New York Life Ins. Co.,* 359 U.S. 437, 449 & n.10 (1959) (Frankfurter, J., dissenting).

22. Supreme Court Rule 10.

23. Id.

24. Lee Epstein et al., *The Supreme Court Compendium: Data, Decisions, and Developments* (Washington, DC: CQ Press, 2007), Table 2–2.

25. Gressman et al., *Supreme Court Practice,* p. 58.

GOLDEN TONGUES
Oral Advocacy Before the Court

1. William H. Rehnquist, "Oral Advocacy," *South Texas Law Review* 27 (1987), p. 289.

2. Shapiro, "Oral Argument in the Supreme Court," p. 23.

3. Ibid.

4. *Chisholm v. Georgia*, 2 U.S. (2 Dall.) 419 (1793).

5. Robert M. Ireland, *The Legal Career of William Pinkney: 1764–1822* (New York: Garland, 1986), p. 54.

6. *Schooner Exchange v. McFaddon*, 7 Cranch 116 (1812).

7. Id. at 136.

8. Ibid.

9. *Republic of Austria v. Altman*, 541 U.S. 677, 688–89 (2004).

10. *Schooner Exchange*, 7 Cranch at 146.

11. Robert Vincent Remini, *Daniel Webster: The Man and His Time* (New York: Norton, 1997), pp. 193–94.

12. Seth P. Waxman, "In the Shadow of Daniel Webster: Arguing Appeals in the Twenty-First Century," *Journal of Appellate Practice & Process* 3 (2001), p. 523.

13. Shapiro, "Oral Argument in the Supreme Court," p. 24.

14. *McCulloch v. Maryland*, 17 U.S. 316 (1819).

15. *Gibbons v. Ogden*, 22 U.S. 1 (1824).

16. *Dartmouth College v. Woodward*, 17 U. S. 518 (1819).

17. H. H. Walker Lewis, *Speak for Yourself, Daniel: A Life of Webster in His Own Words* (Boston: Houghton Mifflin, 1969), p. 62.

18. Kevin T. McGuire, *The Supreme Court Bar: Legal Elites in the Washington Community* (Charlottesville: University Press of Virginia, 1993), p. 15.

19. Lewis, *Speak for Yourself, Daniel*, p. 67.

20. Ibid.

21. Quoted in Everett Pepperrell Wheeler, *Daniel Webster: The Expounder of the Constitution* (New York: G. P. Putnam's Sons, 1905), pp. 29–30.

22. Id. at 31.

23. Lawrence Meir Friedman, *A History of American Law* (New York: Simon & Schuster, 1973), p. 273.

24. Warren, *The Supreme Court in United States History*, vol. 1, p. 471.

25. Quoted in Id. at 473.

26. Shapiro, "Oral Argument in the Supreme Court," p. 23.

27. Ibid.

28. Quoted in G. Edward White and Gerald Gunther, *The Marshall Court and Cultural Change, 1815–1835* (New York: Oxford University Press, 1991), p. 182.

29. The Rules and Orders of the Supreme Court of the United States No. 53 (Dec. Term 1848); Revised Rules of the Supreme Court of the United States No. 26 (1925); Rules of the Supreme Court of the United States No. 44 (1970).

30. Shapiro, "Oral Argument in the Supreme Court," pp. 25, 28.

31. A. H. Garland, *Experience in the Supreme Court of the United States* (Washington, DC: J. Byrne, 1898), p. 5.

32. Id. at 7.

33. A. F. House, "Mr. Justice Field and Attorney General Garland," *Arkansas Law Review* 3 (1949), p. 270.

34. Garland, *Experience in the Supreme Court*, p. 51.

35. Id. at 52.

36. Supreme Court Rule 33(g).

37. Robert H. Jackson, "Advocacy Before the United States Supreme Court," *Cornell Law Quarterly* 37 (1951), p. 2.

38. Guide for Counsel in Cases to be Argued Before the Supreme Court of the United States (Oct. Term 2006), p. 10.

39. Ruth Bader Ginsburg, "Workways of the Supreme Court," *Thomas Jefferson Law Review* 25 (2003), p. 523.

40. William H. Harbaugh, *Lawyer's Lawyer: The Life of John W. Davis* (New York: Oxford University Press, 1973), p. 101.

41. Ibid.

42. Williams, *Thurgood Marshall*, p. 214.

43. Harbaugh, *Lawyer's Lawyer*, p. 50.

44. Id. at 503.

45. Mark Tushnet, "Lawyer Thurgood Marshall," *Stanford Law Review 44* (1992), p. 1285.

46. Ibid.

47. Richard Kluger, *Simple Justice* (New York: Knopf, 1975), p. 672.

48. *New York Statesman*, Feb. 7, 1824, quoted in Warren, *The Supreme Court in United States History*, vol. 1, p. 467.

49. John W. Davis, "The Argument of An Appeal," *American Bar Association Journal* 26 (1940), p. 895.

50. Id. at 897.

51. E. Barrett Prettyman Jr., "The Supreme Court's Use of Hypothetical Questions at Oral Argument," *Catholic University Law Review* 33 (1984), p. 555.

52. Ginsburg, "Workways of the Supreme Court," p. 524.

53. William O. Douglas, *The Court Years, 1939–1975: The Autobiography of William O. Douglas* (New York: Random House, 1980), p. 181.

54. Charles Henry Butler, *A Century at the Bar of the Supreme Court of the United States* (New York: G. P. Putnam's Sons, 1942), pp. 86–87.

55. "Proceedings in Honor of Mr. Justice Brennan," *Harvard Law School Occasional Pamphlet No. 9* (1967), pp. 22–23.

56. John G. Roberts Jr., "Oral Advocacy and the Re-emergence of a Supreme Court Bar," *Journal of Supreme Court History* 30 (2005), p. 70.

CUSTOMS AND TRADITIONS OF THE COURT

1. 5 U.S.C. § 3331.
2. *See* U.S. Const. art. II, § 1 ("Before he enter on the execution of his office, he shall take the following oath or affirmation:—'I do solemnly swear (or affirm) that I will faithfully execute the office of President of the United States, and will to the best of my ability, preserve, protect and defend the Constitution of the United States.' ").
3. 28 U.S.C. § 453; see also 1 Stat. 76.
4. 28 U. S. C. § 456.
5. Office of the Curator, Supreme Court of the United States, "Oaths of Office Taken by the Chief Justices" (2010), available at http://www .supremecourt.gov/about/oath/oathsofthechiefjustices2010.pdf.
6. Office of the Curator, Supreme Court of the United States, "Supreme Court Oath Taking Procedures" (2009), available at http://www .supremecourt.gov/about/oath/oathsproceduresinfosheet2009.pdf.
7. Ibid.
8. Ibid.
9. Ibid.
10. Ibid.
11. Ibid.
12. Ibid.
13. Office of the Curator, Supreme Court of the United States, "Oaths of Office Taken by the Current Court" (2010), available at http://www .supremecourt.gov/about/oath/Oaths_of_the_Current_Court_10-1-2010 .pdf.
14. Tony Mauro, "Change of Venue," *Legal Times*, at 4 (March 2, 2009).
15. Office of the Curator, "Oaths of the Chief Justices," p. 2.
16. Joan Biskupic, "Breyer Takes Court Oath at Chief Justice's Cottage," *Washington Post,* Aug. 4, 1994.
17. Ruth Marcus, "Rehnquist, Scalia Take Their Oaths," *Washington Post*, Sept. 27, 1986.
18. Office of the Curator, "Oaths of the Current Court," p. 2.
19. Ibid.
20. Office of the Curator, Supreme Court of the United States, "Supreme Court Oath Firsts and Other Trivia" (2009), available at http://www .supremecourt.gov/about/oath/supremecourtoathfirstsandtrivia2009.pdf.
21. Brian Lamb, Susan Swain, and Mark Farkas, *The Supreme Court: A C-SPAN Book Featuring the Justices in Their Own Words* (New York: PublicAffairs, 2010), p. 167.

SOME LAUGHS ON THE BENCH

1. Oliver Wendell Holmes, *Collected Legal Papers* (New York: Harcourt, Brace, 1920), p. 292.
2. Jay D. Wexler, "Laugh Track," *Green Bag 2d,* 9 (2005), p. 60.
3. Ibid.
4. Adam Liptak, "So, Guy Walks Up to the Bar, and Scalia Says . . . ," *New York Times,* Dec. 31, 2005.
5. Lamb, Swain, and Parkas, *The Supreme Court,* pp. 114–15.
6. Ryan A. Malphurs, "'People Did Sometimes Stick Things in my Underwear': The Function of Laughter at the U.S. Supreme Court," *Communication Law Review* 10 (2010), p. 48.
7. Adam Liptak, "Study Analyzes Laughs at Supreme Court," *New York Times,* Jan. 24, 2011.
8. Ibid.
9. Malphurs, "The Function of Laughter at the U.S. Supreme Court," p. 48.
10. Id. at 65.
11. Clare Cushman, *Courtwatchers: Eyewitness Accounts in Supreme Court History* (Lanham, MD: Rowman and Littlefield, 2011), pp. 16–17.
12. John Q. Barrett, "A Rehnquist Ode on the Vinson Court," *Green Bag 2d,* 11 (2008), p. 292.
13. Id. at 291.
14. Id. at 301.
15. Id. at 293 and n.17.
16. Glen Elsasser, "Supreme Ironies," *Chicago Tribune,* July 11, 1993.
17. Ibid.
18. Barrett, "A Rehnquist Ode," p. 292.
19. Elsasser, "Supreme Ironies."

LARGER-THAN-LIFE JUSTICES

1. Paul Kens, *Justice Stephen Field: Shaping Liberty from the Gold Rush to the Gilded Age* (Lawrence: University Press of Kansas, 1997), pp. 29–30.
2. *Munn v. Illinois,* 94 U.S. 113, 152 (1876) (Field, J., dissenting).
3. Ibid.
4. Sheldon M. Novick, *Honorable Justice: The Life of Oliver Wendell Holmes* (Boston: Little, Brown, 1989), p. 205.
5. *Buck v. Bell,* 274 U.S. 200 (1927).
6. Novick, *Honorable Justice,* p. 283.
7. *Schenk v. United States,* 249 U.S. 47 (1919).

8. *Abrams v. United States*, 250 U.S. 616 (1919) (Holmes, J., dissenting).
9. Novick, *Honorable Justice*, p. 319.
10. Id. at 263.
11. Id. at 342.
12. James Edward Bond, *I Dissent: The Legacy of Chief Justice James Clark McReynolds* (Fairfax, VA: George Mason University Press, 1992), p. 121.
13. Id. at 123.
14. *West Coast Hotel v. Parrish*, 300 U.S. 379 (1937).
15. Marian C. McKenna, *Franklin Roosevelt and the Great Constitutional War: The Court-packing Crisis of 1937* (New York: Fordham University Press, 2002), p. 419.

GONE BUT NOT FORGOTTEN
Judicial Retirement

1. Judiciary Act of 1869, 16 Stat. 45 (1869); see also Epstein et al., *The Supreme Court Compendium*, p. 44.
2. Minor Myers III, "The Judicial Service of Retired United States Supreme Court Justices," *Journal of Supreme Court History* 32 (2007), p. 47.
3. Pub. L. No. 75–10, 50 Stat. 24; see also Myers, "Judicial Service," p. 47.
4. See ibid.; see also Epstein et al., *The Supreme Court Compendium*, p. 44.
5. Myers, "Judicial Service," p. 47; Epstein et al., *The Supreme Court Compendium*, p. 44.
6. Myers, "Judicial Service," p. 47.
7. Ibid.; see also 28 U.S.C. § 371(c).
8. 28 U.S.C. § 371(a).
9. 28 U.S.C. § 371(e)(1).
10. Artemus Ward, *Deciding to Leave: The Politics of Retirement from the United States Supreme Court* (Albany: State University of New York Press, 2003), p. 186.
11. Id. at 188–89.
12. Id. at 190.
13. Id. at 191.
14. Ibid.
15. Ibid.
16. Ibid. (quoting letter).
17. These figures are derived from Epstein et al., *The Supreme Court Compendium*, pp. 429–35, and updated to include the retirements of Justices Stevens and Souter.
18. Myers, "Judicial Service," p. 48.
19. Ibid.

20. See Epstein et al., *The Supreme Court Compendium*, pp. 429–35.

21. Id. at 429–30.

22. Ward, *Deciding to Leave*, pp. 186–89.

23. Id. at 122–24; see also United States Supreme Court website, "Frequently Asked Questions" (2012), available at http://www.supremecourt.gov/faq_ justices.aspx.

24. G. Edward White, *Justice Oliver Wendell Holmes: Law and the Inner Self* (New York: Oxford University Press, 1995), p. 467; Novick, *Honorable Justice*, p. 375.

25. White, *Justice Holmes*, p. 467.

26. Epstein et al., *The Supreme Court Compendium*, p. 431

27. Ibid.

28. Id. at 430.

29. See Supreme Court Historical Society, "John A. Campbell, 1853–1861," available at http://www.supremecourthistory.org/history-of-the-court/ associate-justices/john-campbell-1853–1861.

30. *The Slaughter House Cases*, 83 U.S. 36 (1873).

31. Epstein et al., *The Supreme Court Compendium*, p. 430.

32. Id. at 431; see also Supreme Court Historical Society, "Charles Evans Hughes, 1930–1941," available at http://www.supremecourthistory.org/ history-of-the-court/chief-justices/charles-evans-hughes-1930–1941.

33. Epstein et al., *The Supreme Court Compendium*, p. 429.

34. Roy M. Mersky and William D. Bader, *The First One Hundred Eight Justices* (Buffalo, NY: W. S. Hein, 2004), p. 20.

35. Epstein et al., *The Supreme Court Compendium*, p. 431.

36. Id. at 434.

37. Id. at 430.

38. Id. at 431; Mersky and Bader, *The First One Hundred Eight Justices*, p. 20.

39. Ward, *Deciding to Leave*, p. 174.

40. Ibid.

41. Ibid.

42. Ibid.

43. Epstein et al., *The Supreme Court Compendium*, p. 430.

44. Id. at 433.

45. Myers, "Judicial Service," p. 48. This number includes Justices Van Devanter, Reed, Burton, Clark, Stewart, Powell, Brennan, Marshall, White, O'Connor, and Souter. See ibid.

46. Ibid.

47. *GTE Sylvania, Inc. v. Continental T.V., Inc.*, 433 U.S. 36 (1977).

48. Myers, "Judicial Service," p. 53.

49. Id. at 54.

50. Id. at 54.
51. Supreme Court Historical Society, "Stanley F. Reed, 1938–1957," available at http://www.supremecourthistory.org/history-of-the-court/associate-justices/stanley-reed-1938-1957.
52. Myers, "Judicial Service," pp. 49–50.
53. Id. at 51.
54. Id. at 54–55.
55. Id. at 55.
56. Patrick T. Hand, "Senior Status,"*Washington Lawyer* (July/August 1993), p. 27 (quoting Justice Powell).
57. Justice O'Connor resignation letter, available at http://www.c-span.org/pdf/resignation_070105.pdf.

SUPREME COURT "FIRSTS"

1. George Pellew, *John Jay* (New York: Chelsea House, 1980), p. 1.
2. Id. at 8.
3. Id. at 235.
4. Irving Dillard, "John Jay," in Friedman and Israel, *The Justices*, vol. 1, pp. 2, 9.
5. Pellew, *John Jay*, pp. 235–37.
6. Id. at 261.
7. William R. Casto, *The Supreme Court in the Early Republic: The Chief Justiceships of John Jay and Oliver Ellsworth* (Columbia: University of South Carolina Press, 1995), pp. 87–88.
8. Dillard, "John Jay," in Friedman and Israel, *The Justices*, vol. 1, p. 17.
9. Leon Friedman, "John Rutledge," in Friedman and Israel, *The Justices*, vol. 1, pp. 23, 35.
10. Ibid.
11. Id. at 36.
12. Ibid.; see also Casto, *The Supreme Court in the Early Republic*, pp. 90–91.
13. Matthew D. Marcotte, "Advice and Consent: A Historical Argument for Substantive Senatorial Involvement in Judicial Nominations," *New York University Journal of Legislation & Public Policy* 5 (2001), p. 541.
14. David J. Garrow, "Mental Decrepitude on the U.S. Supreme Court: The Historical Case for a 28th Amendment," *University of Chicago Law Review*, 67 (2000), p. 999.
15. Casto, *The Supreme Court in the Early Republic*, pp. 93–94.
16. Id. at 92–93.
17. Id. at 95.
18. Ibid.

19. John Bilyeu Oakley and Robert S. Thompson, *Law Clerks and the Judicial Process: Prescriptions of the Qualities and Functions of Law Clerks in American Courts* (Berkeley: University of California Press, 1980), p. 10.

20. Paul R. Baier, "The Law Clerks: Profile of an Institution," *Vanderbilt Law Review* 26 (1973), p. 1130.

21. Ibid.

22. Mark R. Brown, "Gender Discrimination in the Supreme Court's Clerkship Selection Process," *Oregon Law Review* 75 (1996), pp. 362–363 and n.21; Ruth Bader Ginsburg, "The Washington College of Law Founders Day Tribute," *American University Journal of Gender & Law* 5 (1996), p. 1.

23. David J. Danelski, "Lucile Lomen: The First Woman to Clerk at the Supreme Court," *Journal of Supreme Court History* 24 (1999), p. 48.

24. Ginsburg, "Founders Day Tribute," p. 2.

25. Ibid.

26. Data compiled by Supreme Court research librarian Jill Duffy.

27. Kluger, *Simple Justice*, p. 292.

28. Id. at 292–93.

29. Dennis J. Hutchinson, *The Man Who Once Was Whizzer White: A Portrait of Justice Byron R. White* (New York: Free Press, 1998), p. 196.

30. Clare Cushman, *The Supreme Court Justices: Illustrated Biographies, 1789–1995* (Washington, DC: Congressional Quarterly, 1995), p. 537.

31. Phyllis A. Kravitch, "Women in the Legal Profession," *Mississippi Law Journal* 69 (1999), pp. 62–63.

32. Mary L. Clark, "Why Care About the History of Women in the Legal Profession?," *Women's Rights Law Reporter* 27 (2006) p. 60.

33. *Kaiser* v. *Stickney*, 26 L. Ed. 176 (1880).

34. Carl E. Swisher, Carl Brent Swisher. and Paul A. Freund, *History of the Supreme Court of the United States*, vol. 5, *The Taney Period, 1836–64* (New York: Macmillan, 1974), p. 31.

35. See Carl Brent Swisher, *Roger B. Taney* (Hamden, CT: Archon, 1961), pp. 316–17.

36. Id. at 104.

37. *Watts* v. *Indiana*, 338 U.S. 49, 54 (1949).

38. John Henry Hatcher, "Fred Vinson: Congressman from Kentucky. A Political Biography: 1890–1938" (diss. University of Cincinnati, 1967), p. 82.

39. Id. at 98.

40. Id. at 95.

PHOTOGRAPH CREDITS

100 Collection of the Supreme Court of the United States

104 Charley Humberger, National Park Service/Collection of the Supreme Court of the United States

106 Richard Hofmeister, Smithsonian Institution/Collection of the Supreme Court of the United States

108 Michael Evans, The White House/Collection of the Supreme Court of the United States

109 Mary Anne Fackelman, The White House/Collection of the Supreme Court of the United States

110 Franz Jantzen/Collection of the Supreme Court of the United States

114 Ray Lustig/The Washington Post/Getty Images

116 Eileen Colton/Collection of the Supreme Court of the United States

124 Franz Jantzen/Collection of the Supreme Court of the United States

126 Napoleon Sarony, Collection of the Supreme Court of the United States

132 Harris & Ewing/Collection of the Supreme Court of the United States

140 © Yousuf Karsh

153 Steve Petteway/Collection of the Supreme Court of the United States

159 Attributed to Benjamin Falk/Collection of the Supreme Court of the United States

161 Harris & Ewing/Collection of the Supreme Court of the United States

164 AP photo/George Widman

INDEX

———— // ————

NOTE: Bold page numbers refer to picture captions.

ABOUT THE AUTHOR

SANDRA DAY O'CONNOR was born in El Paso, Texas, and raised on the Lazy B Ranch. She attended Stanford University, where she took Wallace Stegner's writing course. She began her public service in Phoenix, and was majority leader of the Arizona Senate before becoming a judge. She is the author of *Lazy B*, a memoir about growing up in the Southwest, and *The Majesty of the Law*, a reflection on American law and life. President Reagan nominated her as Associate Justice of the Supreme Court of the United States, and she served from 1981 to 2006. She served as Chancellor of the College of William & Mary, and is on the board of trustees of the National Constitution Center in Philadelphia.

ABOUT THE TYPE

This book was set in Baskerville, a typeface which was designed by John Baskerville, an amateur printer and typefounder, and cut for him by John Handy in 1750. The type became popular again when The Lanston Monotype Corporation of London revived the classic Roman face in 1923. The Mergenthaler Linotype Company in England and the United States cut a version of Baskerville in 1931, making it one of the most widely used typefaces today.